This book is dedicated to my mother, Ardell, for teaching me that anything is possible. She has been a great mentor and her experience provides a wonderful sounding board in the game of life. Without her guidance and work ethic I would not have become the success I am today.

Copyright © 2009 by Blaine Loomer

All rights reserved. No portion of this book may be reproduced, stored in a retrieval system, or transmitted in any form or by any means—electronic, mechanical, photocopy, recording, scanning, or other—except brief quotations in critical reviews or articles, without the prior written permission of the publisher.

This publication is designed to provide accurate and authoritative information in regard to the subject matter covered, but it is sold with the understanding that the publisher and the author are not engaged in rendering legal, accounting, financial or other professional service. If legal advice or other expert assistance is required, the services of a competent professional person should be sought.

The characters depicted in this publication are fictional. Any similarities to actual persons, living or dead, or actual events are purely coincidental.

Published by Mitchell Publishers Inc.

www.mitchellpublishers.com

ISBN 978-0-9842016-0-0

Printed in the United States of America

CORPORATE BULLSHIT

= A =
SURVIVAL
GUIDE

Blaine Loomer

INTRODUCTION

THROUGHOUT MY YEARS in the corporate world, I have been associated with diverse and interesting groups of individuals. I have consulted with thousands of companies and sat in the boardrooms of some of the largest corporations on the planet. Personalities—both corporate and individual—loom large.

My twenty-plus years in corporate sales have taught me valuable lessons about handling corporate politics, both internal and external. I'd like to share these lessons with you, in an effort to help you deal with some of the unforeseen pitfalls and obstacles you may face in your career. I am still learning, and writing this book has helped me change my approach to life. These tips may help you save time and bring more value to the company, which in turn will bring more value to you. This book is written to help you be your own guardian angel in the world of corporate sharks.

I didn't think *Corporate Bullshit* would be complete without taking a look at some of the characters you may encounter during your career. Scattered throughout are profiles of different personalities, coupled with advice on how to work with them. I have given nicknames to all the players. Some of them may be familiar to you and some may not, but they are all out there. So Beware!

TABLE OF CONTENTS

CORPORATE BULLSHIT

Corporate Accountability	12
CEOs and Boards of Directors	13
Internal Selling	14
Stock Options	16
The Politician	19
Retirement Accounts	21
Lawsuits	23
Compensation Plans	25
Buyouts	27
The Spinster	28
Family-Owned Companies	30
Vacations, Perks, and Trips	32
Making You Rich	33
Cultural Differences	35
The Rooster	36
Decisions	37
Corporate Directives	39
Synergy	40
Financial Reports	41
The Banker	42
Statistics	43
Cash Flow	45
Simplicity	46

The Ripple Effect	47
The Funeral Director	48
Company Policy	49
Start-Ups	50
The Lemonade Stand	51
The Employee–Employer Relationship	53

COLLEAGUE BULLSHIT

Competition	56
Promises	58
Greed	60
Confiding in Others	61
The Tattletale	62
Ability Discrimination	63
Relationships	64
Alliances	66
Trust	69
The Sunshine Pumper	70
Patience	72
Foresight	73
Persuasion	75
The Rumor Mill	78
The Points Shaver	80
Conspiracies	81
Giving Credit Where Credit Is Due	82
Creating Perceptions	84
Taking the Wrong Path	87
The Office Flirt	89
Land Mines	90
Friends and Enemies	92
Changed Attitudes	94

Information	96
The Networker	97
Networking	98
Revenge	99
Safe Communication	101
Blame	103
The Ten-Cent Millionaire	105
Sharing Wealth	106
Big Plans	107
Relationships	108
Set-Ups	109
The Godfather	111
Lies	112
Gifts	114
Corporate Ladder	115
Timing	116
The Repairman	118
Time Theft	119
Industry Relationships	121

YOUR OWN BULLSHIT

Making Money	123
Corporate Direction	125
Personal Investing	127
Promotions and Raises	129
Mr. Negative	130
Titles	131
Negotiation	132
Success	134
Those in Charge	136
The Egomaniac	137

Covering Expenses	139
Adding Value	141
Your Future	142
Self-Preservation	143
The Bomber	144
Delivering News	145
Education	146
Selling Yourself	147
Authority	148
The Taskmaster	149
Handling Conflict	150
Empowerment	151
The Company Line	153
Details	154
The Lawyer	156
Documentation	157
Ideas	158
Balance	160
Warfare	161
The Know-It-All	162
Change	163
Direction	164
Self-Deception	165
Self-Control	166
The Social Worker	167
Intuition	168
Aspirations	169
Travel	170
The Job	171
The Teacher	172

Life	173
Ambition	175
Time Management	176
Personal Direction	177
Father Time	178
Picking an Industry	179
Knowing the Industry	180
Humility	181
Internal Customers	182
Jack-of-All-Trades	183
Automation	184
Positive Influence	185
Prioritizing	186
Return on Investment	187
The Cleaner	188
Follow-Up	189
Communication	190
Planning	191
Deadlines	192
The Wakeboarder	193
Job Satisfaction	194
Motivation	195
Self-Improvement	196
The Superhero	197
Self-Employment	198

CORPORATE ACCOUNTABILITY

It's time to police the corporations

IN YEARS PAST, you could trust upper-level management to act in the best interest of the company and work to ensure its survival. These days I'm not so sure. It seems that personal agendas and personal greed have taken over. Huge bonuses and golden parachutes in the form of exorbitant severance packages are now the norm rather than the exception.

Since corporations aren't willing to police themselves, it's time for us to do it. I propose that we take some of the billions earmarked to bail them out and staff the SEC with auditors who will be embedded in the corporate offices of all publicly traded corporations. If the executives or board members hold a meeting, the auditors will be there to protect the interests of investors and employees. Each quarterly earnings report will be accompanied by an SEC-drafted report to ensure that the company is being a good corporate citizen.

The golden parachutes that management creates for those in its ranks are absurd. Why should incompetent CEOs receive huge amounts of money after they have run the company into the ground? I would like to see "corporate prenuptial agreements." If things don't work out under your management, you leave with what you came with and nothing more.

Sometimes there are foxes in the henhouse

THERE ARE SOME FUNDAMENTAL FLAWS in the way corporations are governed today. In years past, the CEO was assumed to be working in the best interest of the company. It was logical, therefore, for him to be well-rewarded for the company's success. In recent years it seems the exact opposite is true.

Company boards now pay millions of dollars in severance packages to fire members of upper-level management. In doing so they reward these people for essentially running the company into the ground and ruining the stockholders' value. It seems that a corporate CEO can make more money being fired than staying at work.

The most astonishing thing about this dynamic is that these CEOs will get other high-level jobs. How many times have we seen an ex-corporate officer get hired by another company immediately after they came dangerously close to putting their former employer out of business? What are these people thinking?

Beware of used car salesmen

A CHANGE IN CORPORATE DIRECTION often requires a sales job on the part of management to convince employees that the change is a good thing. This is to be expected. Beware, however, if management spends an inordinate amount of time on a sales pitch. If they're hardselling you on the new plan and listing all of the ways it will benefit you, it probably won't.

Management sales pitches are especially rampant when employee compensation packages are changed. Believe me, any changes to comp plans rarely favor the employee. Take an objective look at the new plan independent of the sales pitch and cheerleading that may accompany it. Look for clues in the pitch.

For example, does the plan show partiality to a new product, division, or service offering? If so, take a hard look at where you fall in the big picture of the organization. The sales pitch indicates where the company intends to focus its resources. If you aren't in one of these departments, you may want to consider moving to one of them. The budget money being channeled to these new projects may very well be siphoned from your department. This may not be good news for you or anyone who isn't part of the new plan.

A heavy sales pitch may indicate that management is trying to sell an inferior product, or that the product may not be ready for market. Over the years I have heard a lot of pitches for "great" products, only to find out down the line that the products were disasters. Do some due diligence to see what's "under the hood" before you put either your or the company's reputation on the line.

Don't get the idea that all sales pitches are bad. Just be sure to look beyond the hype and evaluate what's really being said. This kind of scrutiny can give you insight, and can help your career—both short- and long-term.

STOCK OPTIONS

Think twice about those options

COMPANIES USE STOCK OPTIONS TO LURE in good talent and offset high salaries. Company equity can be a great thing, especially if you are with a young company that is experiencing rapid growth. There are, however, a number of things to look out for when you sign up for an option plan. You want to make sure you get the value from them as promised.

Stock options only have value if you can sell them at a profit. In most cases you have to hold them for a long period of time before you can sell them at all. In most cases there is some vesting period before the company issues the options. This is a normal way for the company to protect its investment in you, and to ensure you don't walk out the door as soon as you receive the options.

This is where it gets sticky. You must educate yourself on the goals of the company before you count stock options as a form of compensation. Take a look at the time frame during which you expect to vest and own the stock. Does your time frame for sale match the company's short - and long-term goals? For example, I may have been promised stock in the company and given a vesting time frame of three years. Management's goal may be to sell the company in the next eighteen months. If the sale occurs before my vesting period, I can't sell my shares and they will likely have little or no value. I may not even get them at all, since that decision will be up to the new owners of the company.

I just described what might happen if the company is sold. If the company goes through a capitalization—like an initial public offering (IPO), for example—the timeframe will also have a significant effect on the value of my options. Once again, if the IPO occurs before my options are available to me, I will miss out on what is likely a profound increase in share value. Here's why. In most cases, pre-IPO shares are issued to employees of the company at a significantly reduced rate, say $1. At the time of the IPO, the price to the public will be much higher, say $10. In this case those who are able to sell their shares will realize a $9 per share profit. Since my shares are not available to me until after the IPO—when I am vested—the shares will most likely be issued to me at the then-market price of $10. I will now have to wait for a significant increase in market price in order to realize a profit. This may take years, or it may never happen at all.

You can protect yourself. First, make sure that all equity promises are in writing. Your agreement should include language that allows you to be immediately vested and able to exercise any shares promised if the company is sold or capitalized.

Unfortunately, some companies promise you equity and stock options but have no intention of delivering either. Again, get equity promises in writing. If there are no shares available because the company is currently privately owned, have management include some percentage of ownership in your employment contract. Keep all vesting periods as short as possible. Often, those who joined the company early and helped make it a success aren't around when it's time to cash out. Make sure there is a provision in your employment agreement that allows you keep any equity you have, even if you are fired. There are companies out there that will ride you for everything you're worth, then fire you before the big payout. Always remember if it is too good to be true it probably isn't.

THE POLITICIAN

"I know how to play the game"

I MISS THE GOOD OL' DAYS, when promotions were awarded based on merit. It seems that practice has fallen by the wayside in favor of office politics. The Politician gets the job—you know, the person who is in the boss's office every five minutes, declaring her indispensable worth.

I guess there's a little politician in all of us, but some people take it too far. They do anything to win the political game. The Politician usually gets sucked into this lifestyle over a period of years, and before they know it they are consumed with company politics. They get so focused on the game that they forget about the job at hand. Their life becomes the *next* job, the *next* promotion, the *next* project. They spend little or no time fulfilling their current responsibilities.

This behavior must cost corporations millions—if not billions—of dollars in productivity every year.

So how can you protect yourself from the Politician and earn the promotion you deserve? First, evaluate the boss. If the boss has a huge ego, then the Politician is tough to beat. Politicians excel at stroking egos and kissing a lot of ass to get what they want. If the boss isn't an Egomaniac, he will soon tire of the grandstanding. The Politician will defeat herself.

Once you have determined the boss's motivating factors, you can adapt your behavior to combat the Politician without losing focus on your job. The best way to do this is to state facts. Documentation and accountability to the Politician are like kryptonite to Superman. Politicians can't spread a lot of bullshit if there is documentation that proves who is really doing the work. Create a paper trail. Save all of your emails and voicemails, if possible. You may need them for later reference.

Politicians abuse email. They ask you to forward documents to them for review, then they send them on to the boss without your knowledge. They like to create the perception that they did the work. A favorite tactic is to reply to you—cc'ing the boss, of course—but taking credit for your work. Don't fall into this trap! Take advantage of software packages' password protection features. Make sure the information stream to the boss flows directly from you. Don't give the Politician an opportunity to put her name on work that originated with you.

By the way, it never hurts to brag about yourself a little bit. Make yourself known. Establish your value in the organization. Healthy politicking may serve you well.

Don't count on the company

WE ALL INTEND TO RETIRE SOMEDAY. With a few notable exceptions, most company-funded defined benefit plans—sometimes called pensions—are nonexistent. You and I have to fund our own retirements if we expect to end our careers with more than just basic Social Security.

Defined benefit plans have been replaced by defined contribution plans, such as a 401(k). If you're wise, you invest in the plan every paycheck. If you're lucky, your company may match a portion of your contributions.

A 401(k) is a good tool for saving money. It is tax deferred—not tax exempt. *You will pay tax on this money at some point.* Even so, the tax advantages encourage us to contribute.

These retirement accounts have channeled billions of dollars into the stock market that otherwise wouldn't be there. The fat cats on Wall Street will figure out a way to keep your money if you're not savvy.

A few guidelines can help you hang on to your investment. First, know where it's going and how it is distributed within your 401(k) account. (By the way, do you even look at your statements? Maybe you should!) Age equals the level of risk you should take. If you are close to retirement, take less risk. If you are younger, you may want to take more. Typically, higher-risk investments have more opportunity for a larger return over time. But remember, they also carry the greatest potential for loss.

If you decide to invest your 401(k) contributions in your employer's stock, make damn sure the company is viable. Ever heard of Enron? Lots of hardworking people—who believed their employer's brand of bullshit—suffered heavy losses when the company went under. Very risky!

LAWSUITS

No one is watching the house

LAWSUITS ARE FILED FOR MANY REASONS—not all of them to settle legitimate claims. Some are intended to reduce competition in the marketplace—to stop or stall the growth of a competitor. Companies' financial resources are drained when they are forced to defend themselves against legal action. Some lawsuits have no foundation—and those filing them know it. Corporations sue a competitor to aggravate them, or to create doubt in the marketplace. And of course, the news is full of stories of everyday people looking for an easy payout from an unsuspecting victim.

Turbulent times on Wall Street often tempt shareholders to seek recourse through the courts. In many cases, their efforts are fruitless. The investors share a common misconception that if an individual or corporation does something wrong or dishonest, they, as an offended party, will have some legal recourse to fix the problem or be made whole. Often, nothing is further from the truth.

Corporations spend billions to manufacture laws that shield them from legal action, especially in the investment and capital markets. When all else fails, they can file for corporate bankruptcy, and in a single penstroke, they can wipe out shareholders and bondholders, while keeping their core interests intact. Some corporations—and their well-paid advisors—use bankruptcy as a tool to transfer wealth from us to them.

If you invest in a public company, and the powers-that-be avail themselves of the current bankruptcy laws, you will likely lose all the value of your stock. The current owners—including you—will be forced out. Management, on the other hand, will garner praise for their restructuring plan. Their elimination of company debt will make the company, which you no longer own a part of, much more profitable in the future.

Don't think for one minute that the Securities and Exchange Commission (SEC) or any other government agency is "watching the house." If you believe otherwise, put your money under your mattress. In most cases of investment loss—fraudulent or not—lost money is lost money and you will have no legal recourse to get it back. In the few cases that have been paid out, most of the settlement money went to class action law firms; investors wound up with a few pennies on the dollar.

Protect yourself from this legal mess by staying out of it. Lawsuits are not the answer. Do your best to do business with reputable people; work hard for your living. But recognize that you do business with individuals and corporations at your own peril.

Stick around—it'll change

EVERY YEAR, GOOD CORPORATE CITIZENS look to see where they can cut expenses in order to improve the bottom line. Most companies' largest expenditure is labor, so this area of the budget always comes under meticulous scrutiny. Whether you know it or not, your comp plan is reviewed every year.

It's not uncommon for employees to receive some type of annual cost-of-living increase. Cost-of-living increases are not pay increases. Rather, they are an acknowledgement by your employer that the amount of money you spend for basic goods and services increases year over year. It's their attempt to help you meet those changing costs. If you want to increase your salary, you must ask for a raise in pay over and above a cost-of-living increase.

If you are in sales or a similar performance-related role, you may see a complete restructuring of your comp plan as frequently as every year. Changes in comp plans are especially prevalent in industries that have recurring revenue streams such as insurance, manufacturing, and service companies. An adjustment is not necessarily a bad thing, but do pay attention to the sales pitch. (See *Internal Selling*.) If management spends a lot of time selling the comp plan to you, you damn well better take a hard look at what it is and how it affects your income. Compare the plan to last year's numbers and see how it plays out.

Keep in mind that comp plans are designed to influence employees' behavior. For example, a company may want to expand its business into a different industry. This strategy will likely give birth to a comp plan that is more favorable toward growing business in the new industry than it is toward solidifying existing business.

When you evaluate any comp plan, pay attention to detail to make sure you are not taking a step back. In some cases, your company may simply be increasing its margins. Stay on top of it and don't let them do this at your expense. Anything you give up, you won't likely get back!

Mergers & Acquisitions affect you

MERGERS AND ACQUISITIONS ARE A MAINSTAY of corporate strategy. Eliminating competition, increasing market share, and gaining efficiency are but a few reasons why your company might get bought out.

Why should you care about a merger or a buyout? Because once the two companies become one, the new entity will achieve its efficiency goals by consolidating redundant tasks. Management may tell you that the company is expanding, but it's obvious they are shrinking two companies into one. Do some research. If the acquiring company has a department like yours, then your job is in jeopardy.

But don't panic. This is a great chance for you to evaluate your position with your current employer and review how you're progressing on your career path. If you are dissatisfied, this might be the eye-opener you need to find work with a different company or in a different field. You will spend in total almost a third of your life working, so if at all possible, do something you enjoy. Keep an open mind and see what comes down the road. You never know—this may be the opportunity you've been waiting for.

THE SPINSTER

"I'm doing this for you"

GOING BACK THROUGH HISTORY there has always been the Spinster, from the first person to sell a bottle of elixir in the Old West to the modern millionaire who hawks his product on late-night infomercials. The goal of the Spinster is to convince his audience that whatever he is doing or selling is a great idea. "Spin" can be a good thing if you need to motivate the troops or get the team fired up at half-time. However, when spin is attached to a personal agenda, it can be very dangerous to those around it.

The Spinster knows there is power in numbers. The more people he can recruit, the faster his agenda will be executed. Ask yourself who is doing the spinning and why. The person doing the spinning usually stands to benefit the most.

Spin is easy to recognize as it is typically delivered with intense enthusiasm. The Spinster tries to convince you that what they are doing is for your benefit to the point that they are sacrificing themselves for you. They may say, "If I do this for you, I'm losing money," or, "I'm not asking you to do this for me." Classic statements like these help the Spinster create the perception that they have nothing to gain, which adds credibility to their story.

There are other ways to work spin. The Spinster may indeed not benefit directly from helping you. Their payoff may be in convincing you to help someone else, who will in turn help them. The bottom line is, if someone is overly enthusiastic about assisting you or putting money in your pocket, watch out!

FAMILY-OWNED COMPANIES

Don't expect to be treated like family unless you *are* family

IF YOU WORK FOR A FAMILY-OWNED COMPANY, you face a unique set of challenges. The saying "Blood is thicker than water" is particularly evident in the business world.

One big hurdle is opportunity for advancement. You may discover that upper-level jobs are reserved for family only, and you have gone as far as you can. Just when you thought you were going to get that promotion, the absent son-in-law or brother-in-law appears on the scene. There isn't a whole lot you can do about this and it will likely be a big surprise to you since these types of discussions don't occur within the office. There is always the option of marrying into the family, but marrying in could turn out to be the hardest job you've ever had.

Another thing you will have a hard time with is compensation. Every dollar a family-owned company gives you is a dollar out of the family's pocket. Keep this in mind when you review your comp plan. It will likely be much lower than what a larger or public company might offer you.

You may never gain equity in the company. Distant relatives and other extended family members you've never even heard of will do their best to keep "outsiders" from sharing ownership. They no doubt recognize the company's value, and will be lining up for a piece of the pie when the owner either retires or dies. They certainly don't want you getting a share of their inheritance, even though they may have never darkened the door of the company or done anything to make it a success.

Finally, the person who started the company will likely continue to work there until they physically can't make it to the office anymore. So if you have ever been promised any ownership in a family company you had better hope you are in the will (and even then your share may be contested). Otherwise, you'll be working for the brother-in-law you don't like who has no experience at all in your industry.

Family-owned companies are good stepping-stones, but don't count on them to build your wealth. Either start your own business or go to work for a public company where the comp plans are more robust and there is an opportunity to own shares.

Say no to working vacations

TIME OFF FROM YOUR JOB IS ESSENTIAL for your survival in the business world. Taking a few days to decompress and remove yourself from the day-to-day routine gives you a fresh perspective on your career and your life. No one ever won an award for taking the fewest number of vacation days.

When you take your vacation, *take your vacation!* Remove yourself from the job completely. Don't offer to check e-mail and voicemail while you are away. I have made this mistake and I can tell you if you do it, you might as well have stayed at work.

A lot of companies offer rewards and perks like club trips or weekend getaways. Although these are great and can be a lot of fun, they are not vacations. They are still about the company and you will still be working. You'll just be out of the office.

MAKING YOU RICH

Becoming wealthy is your responsibility

MOST OF US WOULD LOVE TO HAVE the wealth and power that we see in today's media. Companies use our desire to be wealthy to their advantage all of the time. Here is a simple maxim to live by: No one but you is in the business of making you rich!

Any company or individual who claims they will make you wealthy is typically not selling what you think they are. We have all seen the late-night infomercials on TV and the get-rich-quick schemes people have come up with. If these programs are so lucrative, they sure as hell wouldn't be telling *you* about it! They would be doing it themselves! So what are they really selling? They are selling the *idea* of wealth and in most cases they make their money selling the very products they claim will make you wealthy.

Unfortunately, these tactics have filtered their way into what I call the legitimate business world. More and more companies are taking the no-cost-employee approach, claiming that selling their product will make you rich so there is no need for them to pay you.

Beware of companies that pitch these get-rich-while-you-sit-on-the-beach schemes, especially those that require you to invest heavily up front. They couldn't care less if the Internet terminal or point-of-purchase machine they sold you generates even one dollar. They aren't selling you a business; they are selling you hardware, which they claim will make you rich. That's where they make their money. You're still going to have to work really hard for any payoff.

These are high-volume businesses. Instead of hiring employees to go out and sell two million units of their product, they go out and recruit a million people to sell two units. In the meantime a few million people make a few dollars and those who own the company make hundreds of millions peddling their recruits a warehouse full of cheap crap.

Bottom line: understand your employer's motivation. Make sure you are an employee and not their customer. Keep your personal investment to a minimum. If someone asks you to make a large investment of time and money but gives you nothing in return, you are their customer, not their employee. They are making their money from *you*, not the people to whom you are selling.

CULTURAL DIFFERENCES

A norm in one culture may be totally unacceptable in another

YOU PROBABLY ENGAGE DIRECTLY or indirectly with different cultures around the globe. Every day, American workers feel the effects of these "outside" influences.

As the world gets smaller and smaller, we notice cultural differences more and more. Don't be too quick to dismiss a business practice that may seem strange to you. Keep an open mind toward this alternative way to do business. Try to understand the practice and how it might benefit you, your company, your customers, and your fellow employees.

And if you must interact with workers from other countries, it's wise to research their country's business practices. Doing so will streamline your interactions with them significantly.

THE ROOSTER

"I like the fence"

ROOSTERS ARE INTERESTING characters. I call them Roosters for two reasons: They seem to want to crow a lot about themselves, and they also like to sit on the fence to avoid making decisions.

The Rooster is a bit of an egomaniac. This affects his ability to make decisions. If a Rooster makes a poor one, it's a huge bruise to his ego. At some point he may have to admit that he was wrong. This fear of imperfection keeps the Rooster on the fence; he makes no decision at all. If he is lucky, someone else will make it, or the decision will make itself if he waits long enough. Either way, the Rooster's passive approach allows him to maintain a level of deniability.

The Rooster is always quick to assign blame. He seems to be more concerned with finding out who is responsible for the problem and less interested in fixing it and finding its cause (not that he could fix anything anyway—then he would have to make a decision). The Rooster prefers to ignore problems and hopes they go away.

There are two things you can do if you have to work with a Rooster. Either force him to make a decision, or tear down the fence and watch him run around aimlessly. Whichever choice you make, you will need a lot of patience.

DECISIONS

Pay attention to how decisions are made

EVERY DAY YOU MAKE DECISIONS that affect your personal life as well as your professional life. Corporations are no different. Someone in the company has to figure out which path to take. How decisions are made speaks volumes about the company and its management team.

Some people can't make decisions because they fear making the wrong one. These Roosters sit on the fence for so long that someone or some event ends up making the decision for them. This gives them deniability when the shit hits the fan. I classify politicians as Roosters—you'll never get a decision out of them. If they do make a decision it is accompanied by a long list of conditions that must remain true in order for them to take responsibility for the outcome, once again, giving them an excuse if the decision turns out to be a poor one. When you execute a decision made by a Rooster, be prepared to accept the consequences if things go wrong. Whenever possible try to get their decision—if they've made one—in writing so you can protect yourself.

I classify decisions into two categories: short-term and long-term. Short-term decisions are made day-to-day and carry little risk. These can range from how much a company is going to produce in a single day all the way down to where you may be going for lunch. The point is that these types of decisions are made quickly, as you might expect.

Long-term decisions usually have a significant effect on the company and carry high risk. They are strategic, and include initiatives like developing a new product or taking a new direction by selling off a division. Moves like these often require multiple discussions and a lengthy period of time to choose the correct course.

How decisions are made tell you a lot about the company and its management team. Roosters are frustrating to work with. It is easier to work with people who are decisive and tend to evaluate information quickly. Unlike a Rooster, a decisive person is less concerned with self-protection than in getting the job done. They are likely to go with the decision that carries the least risk for them. Take time to understand their thought processes and try to evaluate their goals. The two of you may very well be going in the same direction and can help each other.

Like individuals, companies have decision-making styles. Pay special attention to the timeframe. Long-term decisions being made on short-term bases are red flags, especially if the decisions make no sense. When you see this, ask yourself what event may have triggered the decision. It could signal that the company is running low on resources or that there may be an impending buyout. Whatever the reason, something significant is behind it.

CORPORATE DIRECTIVES

It doesn't necessarily come from the top

WE ASSUME THAT ALL CORPORATE directives are issued by upper-level management, but this assumption is not always true. Often lower-level managers blame their own unpopular decisions on their superiors, even though the executives had nothing to do with them. Playing the blame game allows lower-level managers to stay popular with their employees while still getting their jobs done.

Sometimes lower-level managers prerelease critical information in order to create havoc within the company. For example, they may be privy to a directive to cut employees. A manager who doesn't agree with this decision may leak the news. This creates a wave of complaints that upper-level management has to deal with and may in fact force them to change directions even before they have had a chance to execute the strategy.

Just because someone tells you "It comes from the top" doesn't mean it does.

SYNERGY

Do your best to get along

COMPANY DEPARTMENTS ARE fundamentally different both in personality and function. An accountant is not an engineer is not a salesperson. Each personality or role has its own strengths and might well be at the top of its game in the organization.

What corporations desire is synergy among departments. This helps them gain maximum efficiency, keep costs under control, and minimize conflict. For example, Engineering may believe that unless they produce great products, the Sales team has nothing to sell. Sales might argue that without their efforts, there would be no revenue and the engineers would be unemployed. In reality both teams are right and equally important to the success of the company. Each role's perspective is valid.

You can combat differences in opinion by having departments work together as one team. If possible, have your teams switch jobs or shadow a coworker for a day. This might give them a whole different perspective on another person's job and help them gain appreciation for what the other departments do. At the end of the day, you must find a way to get along.

FINANCIAL REPORTS

Numbers count

CORPORATE DECISIONS ARE financially motivated. And why shouldn't they be? After all, companies must make money to stay in business. Financial reports can be confusing and can say a variety of things. Have a basic understanding of what the data says if you intend to be successful in business.

Numbers can be interpreted many different ways. I have seen multiple interpretations of the same report depending on which department head was looking at it and what their motivation was.

A sure way to tell if someone is manipulating the numbers is if the numbers always agree with their agenda. No matter what department you are in or what company you work for, this almost never happens. Even if *most* of the numbers support their plan, rarely will *all* of them support it.

Learn how to interpret the numbers. Doing so will help you make better sense of corporate direction and make you more adaptable to change. Evaluation of your own performance or department against the numbers will also help you make sure you are aligned with the company's direction.

THE BANKER

"I'll keep an eye on the money"

THE BANKER IS ALWAYS ON THE LOOKOUT for numbers and wants to keep an eye on the money. She is curious to know her colleagues' salaries and all the intimate details of the company financials, even though having access to data of this nature is not part of her job. If she can't ferret out this information, she feels like she is being slighted—left out of the loop.

Be careful what you share with the Banker. The information will likely be spread around the company. God forbid that someone makes a mistake and the Banker gets wind of it. Everyone in the company will be on alert until the error is corrected.

STATISTICS

The numbers may be designed to mislead you

NUMBERS DON'T LIE, but the people who create them may! Nearly every time an individual or a group of people tries to make a point, they throw out statistics to support it. In most cases we should be less concerned about what the statistics do tell us, and more concerned with what the statisticians don't tell us.

Demographics, sample size, and method of gathering data are a few of the factors that go into the process of developing statistics. How those factors are framed affects what companies tell us. The statistics may be legit, but may be incomplete. Key information may have been left out. For example, we have all heard TV ads tout statements like: "Four out of five people surveyed recommend Product X." What if they only asked five people? Do five people provide a legitimate representative sample of Product X's users? What if the five people they asked had never heard of the product, so none of them recommended it? Does this mean it is a bad product? Probably not.

Another common approach that is used—especially by special interest groups—is to throw out shockingly large numbers. I heard an example of this the other day on one of the local news stations. The story was about how many American children are not covered by some form of health insurance. The statement was made that there are 80 million American children under the age of 18 without health insurance. Sounds alarming, doesn't it?

If we just think about that statement for a minute we can see that we have been duped into believing something that is not true. Since there are only about 300 million people in the United States to begin with, the total number under 18 years old can't be more than 70 or 80 million. Just for the sake of argument, let's say the total number of people under 18 is 80 million, or around 25–30 percent of the total population. In order for this alarming statistic to be true, that would mean that no person under the age of 18 is covered by health insurance of any kind. Sorry, but I don't buy that one.

The point here is, don't believe everything you hear just because someone throws out a statistic to support it. If you add up all of the things that special interest groups tell us will kill us—auto accidents, smog, secondhand smoke, global warming—the human race should have been extinct fifty years ago. Use a little practical deduction before you accept any statistic as fact.

CASH FLOW

Don't assume the company can afford it

IT IS A COMMON BELIEF among employees that the company has a seemingly endless supply of cash. I wish I had a dollar for every time I've heard, "The company can afford it!"

In reality the company has money coming in and going out every month, just like you and me. This is called *cash flow*. You have a salary or wage that you are paid every month, and you pay your bills from that salary. If you regularly have more bills than salary, you will become insolvent and go bankrupt. Your company is no different. The company's "salary" is the monthly revenue it receives. If the company has more bills than salary, it too will go bankrupt.

Just because the company has a greater volume of money coming in and out than you do doesn't mean there is an endless supply of it.

SIMPLICITY

Don't complicate things

KEEP THINGS SIMPLE. This is one of the best rules to live by in the corporate jungle. It's no wonder people don't have any time and have to work late these days. They're just trying to sort through the policies and procedures that have grown up around them.

Propagate the philosophy of simplicity throughout the company and everyone's life will run much smoother. If you have to write a corporate policy, make sure it is clear, concise, and easy to understand. Complicated policies are hard to develop, hard to execute, and hard to administer. If you can't understand the policy, how can you teach it to someone else and expect him to follow it?

THE RIPPLE EFFECT

It's not all about you

ALL OF US HAVE A TENDENCY to do what is best for us without considering how our actions may affect other people or departments in the company. Just because something is easier for you doesn't mean that it's easier for everyone. Subtle changes that benefit you may create havoc through the company as a whole.

All parts of an organization are connected in some way. For example, a change in expense policy for the sales staff may make it easier for Sales but create lots of problems for Accounting. Your small tweak may require major alterations to Accounting's software and processing systems. So take the time to evaluate the effect a change will have on other parts of the organization. Ask the other players to weigh in. Improved efficiency and cost savings efforts are good, as long as they don't impair processes or inflate costs somewhere else.

THE FUNERAL DIRECTOR

"It's all doom and gloom"

SOME PEOPLE LIVE ON NEGATIVE ENERGY and are motivated by crisis. Drama drives their day. I call these individuals Funeral Directors.

Funeral Directors usually have ample time to complete their assigned tasks. But for whatever reason, they procrastinate or otherwise delay progress until there is a crisis and something "just has to be done." Any task you give them will eventually become the "end of the world" until it is accomplished.

When you work with a Funeral Director, pad the schedule. Make sure that the deadline you assign them is earlier than the actual deadline. This will ensure that their crisis does not become yours.

COMPANY POLICY

Try never to say, "It's our policy"

WE KNOW WE MUST ABIDE by our company's corporate policy—its laws to live by, so to speak. The place where most companies cross the line is when they create policy and impose it on someone else, mainly their customers.

How many times have you been on the phone with customer service and all they want to do is tell you about their corporate policy? Do you really care what their policy is? Does their policy help you solve your problem? In most cases the answer is no.

Policies, like contracts, primarily benefit those who create them. Otherwise they wouldn't exist. If you are in a position to create policy, consider the impact they have on your customers, both internal and external. If at all possible, allow enough flexibility in them that you won't alienate your customers.

START-UPS

Get in on the ground floor

IT SOUNDS GREAT TO GET INVOLVED in a start-up company. We've all heard the success stories of riches beyond dreams. We hope that someday our story will be told in a nationally recognized business magazine or some other forum that will bring us fame or recognition.

There are some things you need to know before you invest time or money in a start-up. Make sure you understand the motivation of the owner. In many cases, entrepreneurs intend to sell the company—or parts of it—within a certain timeframe or after they've achieved a milestone event or revenue target. This may create a problem for you if you are looking for long-term employment. Remember, everything is for sale for the right amount of money, so the company could be sold at any time.

Beware of promises of ownership or equity in the company. Make sure you get all promises in writing, or they may have very little value later. The person who claims to have built the company probably has a big ego, and might want to keep all of the revenue when it is sold. People who start companies forget that there are a lot of people around them who also sacrificed to make the business a success. Often, the coworkers worked as hard as the owner did.

The only way to guarantee ownership in a start-up is to be the owner.

THE LEMONADE STAND

The company might give you a lemon

IF YOU HAVE EVER HEARD anyone say, "I thought the best way to get your group to do something extraordinary was to tell them it couldn't be done," then you have been a customer at the lemonade stand.

This little-known tactic is sometimes used by upper-level management when they are looking for drastic changes in company structure, products, or practices, or when they need fresh ideas. Typically, very few people are aware of the true agenda, and even they may not expect a definable result.

This is how it works. You may be given a directive to make extensive changes to a seemingly dead product, but you won't be given much guidance. You will corral the company's most creative minds into a brainstorming session to figure out what you can do with it. You are in a way conducting a team-building exercise to rally everyone to solve the problem, which is, "The company gave us these lemons and asked us to make lemonade."

Management's true objective may be to launch a new product or to identify the outstanding employees in a group. It is likely that the initial directive given to you is just a cover story to keep everyone focused on the goal at hand and work objectively without personal agendas.

These plans can be very complex or very simple and extremely difficult to decode since so few people know the true agenda. If a member of management is in the meeting and participating in the brainstorming session with you, you can be certain that they are not in on the game.

THE EMPLOYEE–EMPLOYER RELATIONSHIP

Create realistic expectations

THE DYNAMIC OF THE EMPLOYEE–EMPLOYER relationship always surprises me. In most cases these relationships deteriorate because neither side set reasonable expectations from the beginning.

Think about the interview process. If you are an employer and you are impressed with a candidate's qualifications, you want them to work for you. It's human nature to make the job sound better than it really is. If you are an employee, you may be impressed with the company, and you may want to work there. It's also human nature for you to make yourself sound more competent or skilled than you really are. After a few months of working together, the relationship starts to go sour, and neither party can figure out why. My theory is that things fell apart because the relationship was built on bullshit—from both sides.

During the interview, the employer may have said that little or no overtime was required. In practice, the employee has to stay late two or three nights a week just to keep up. In the interview, the employee may have expressed a willingness to put in sixty hours a week, but in practice she refuses to work more than forty.

Unrealistic expectations benefit no one. Be truthful and forthcoming in talking about what you want from each other. It's better to realize early on—preferably before you hire or are hired—that expectations don't match, and there could never be a solid relationship between you.

COLLEAGUE BULLSHIT

COMPETITION

They'll stop at nothing

COMPETITION IS BRUTAL. People compete for everything these days: jobs, schools, business success, wealth, and status. Here are a couple of tips on what the competition might try and how you can avoid their traps.

In most cases the competition doesn't work to make their company look good. Instead, they try to make you look bad. In fact, the more worthy an adversary you become, the more desperate their attacks will be. This approach isn't effective in the long term, but with today's lust for instant gratification it seems to be a preferred tactic.

Anytime I hear of a salesperson running down their competition, I take a close look at the competitor's product. I figure they must be getting attacked for a reason.

If they can't tear down your company, they will inevitably come after you personally with a few well-planned attempts at character assassination. I have seen them all. For example, I heard of a salesperson who started a rumor that his counterpart at his competitor had contracted HIV. It didn't take long for this rumor to spread around the industry. Since this was in the early days of AIDS, no one wanted the "infected" sales rep in their office. The rumor-starter won orders by default. This benefited him in the short-term, but once his tactic was discovered, he was fired.

The point is that your competition will stop at nothing to win, so be prepared. You may be inclined to fight fire with fire but that is one of the worst ways to handle these attacks. Stick to a positive approach and try to convince your potential customer that you or your product is the best choice. If you do anything less, you'll just be in the middle of a pissing match that neither one of you may win.

PROMISES

A verbal promise is like a bad check

MAKING A PROMISE is a way of influencing someone else's behavior. Promises are often made for noble reasons. They may be used to convince people to take action, to motivate them, or to eliminate their apprehension about a task or situation.

We've all been disappointed at least once by a promise-maker. More often than not, we're surprised when someone actually keeps his word. This is true both in and out of the office.

How do you make sure you receive what you were promised? First of all, take a minute to ask yourself, "Was I truly promised something?" You may discover that you were not. Some individuals are skillful at implying a promise without actually pledging anything. For example, "This company will be worth a lot of money some day and I want you to be around for that." The implication is that you will benefit directly from the company's success. In reality, you will have the privilege of watching the promise-maker walk away with a big fat check.

Some people say whatever it takes to get you to help them succeed; they have no intention of making good on their promise. The only protection you have against this is to do whatever you can to get their promise in writing. You won't be able to force them to honor their word, but at least you will be able to produce proof of the promise. This will remove any doubt when it comes time for you to "collect," and it will minimize their ability to deny what was said. Getting it in writing is all the more important if what has been pledged carries real value for you.

GREED

Never underestimate another guy's greed

WHEREVER THERE IS MONEY and wealth, there is greed—the insatiable need for more. *More* is a powerful motivator for a lot of people, and for some, it can become a dangerous obsession.

Greed is not necessarily a bad thing. A little bit of it helps us take care of ourselves and our families. Where would you be if you never wanted more of anything?

The question is: How do we harness greed for our benefit? Take stock in yourself and those around you. A greedy person is typically self-centered and stops at nothing to satisfy his need for more. Don't get in the way of this motivation or you will become a sacrificial lamb. Instead, try to use this motivation to your advantage.

Once you have identified the greedy, put a few bucks in their pockets. If you assign them tasks that are tied to financial reward, you can bet the tasks will get completed. Soon, your greedy coworker will be executing your agenda.

CONFIDING IN OTHERS

Watch your back

PROTECT THE INTELLECTUAL PROPERTY of You, Inc. Information is power and people try to obtain information from anywhere at any time. Be careful with whom you discuss company topics, as this information may be used against you, even by someone who claims to be your friend.

The after-office happy hour is a grazing ground for those looking for information. An innocent conversation after work over a couple of beers can easily sink you on Monday morning if what you have said gets into the wrong hands. People pump you for data, claiming to be on your side of a particular issue, only to change their tune when they get back to the office on Monday. If the information they have gleaned will in some way help them, they will use it.

The best way to protect yourself is to shut up and listen. You may be the one who learns something that helps You, Inc.

THE TATTLETALE

"I'll go to the boss"

DO YOU EVER WONDER how the boss finds out about everything? Odds are it is through the Tattletale. Just as some people strive to be the bearers of good news, the Tattletale loves to share bad news—as long as the bad news is about somebody else and not them.

The only thing you can trust about a Tattletale is that they will disclose any information you tell them if doing so can give them a leg up in the company. Anything you say to them can and will be used against you.

The Tattletale does have some value, however. If you want to spread information, just tell it to them and ask them to keep the communication confidential. They won't be able to resist the temptation, and your message will quickly spread throughout the company network.

ABILITY DISCRIMINATION

You may be too good

MOST PEOPLE THINK DISCRIMINATION applies only to race or sex. There is another form of discrimination that goes unchecked. People who have great ability and are doing a good job are often discriminated against because they pose a threat to a superior, they may be getting in the way of someone else's promotion, or they may be raising the productivity of a group to such high standards that their fellow employees are angry.

In some cases, managers favor an employee who is less competent than they are because they fear for their own job if a more competent person is allowed to advance. They may also go out of their way to discredit a good employee so others will not know how advantageous it is to have that person on their team.

If this is happening to you, you are not alone. The best way to fight ability discrimination is by blowing your own horn. Don't assume you are getting any credit for the good job you are doing. Your boss is probably taking credit for your accomplishments, especially if he is an Egomaniac. Maneuver past coworkers who are trying to hold you back. Make your presence known. As more people throughout the organization understand your contributions, the less likely it will be for adversaries to prevent you from advancing.

RELATIONSHIPS

Strive for authentic relationships

YOU MUST MAINTAIN professional relationships in the workplace. You need to interact with your fellow employees in an efficient and productive manner. Still, use caution and make sure the relationships you establish are genuine.

If someone wants to advance a personal agenda, they will figure out with whom they need to establish a relationship and they'll aggressively go after it. You may be their target, especially if you've been working at the same company for a long period of time. If a fellow coworker suddenly goes out of their way to help you out or acts like they're your new best friend, watch out. They want something. Keep them at arm's length until you know what they're up to. There is a good chance that they may have some information about an upcoming promotion or career opportunity that you haven't heard about yet.

This is not only true of coworkers at your level but of subordinates as well. A subordinate may start sucking up to you because they need your help or your recommendation to get a promotion. Once they've gotten what they want from you, they'll be gone, sucking up to the next person who can help them along.

Be aware of individual agendas. With any new relationship, ask yourself what value you can provide for this newfound "friend." If you quickly identify something they want, you will have identified their agenda, and you'll be able to make decisions that are in your best interest, not theirs.

ALLIANCES

There is strength in numbers

SOME ALLIANCES ARE CREATED among people who have similar opinions and goals. Some are created out of necessity: "If you help me, I will help you." Alliances created out of necessity are dangerous and may bring together very unlikely parties. Two or more people can create massive chaos and start a lot of fires that may be nearly impossible to put out.

Groups are more effective than individuals in executing an agenda because the more people involved, the more credible the plan. A group is also better able to force a plan through different departments, departments you may or may not have control over.

Don't assume you or your business activity will be unaffected because the allies operate outside of your department. They may have recruited an information broker from your group that feeds information to them. Or perhaps you are an unwilling or unknowing accomplice to their agenda.

Allies may be internal or external. Some groups recruit external allies to help them. In these cases their goal is to ruin your reputation outside of the company. For example, the group may recruit a customer to complain about you or create the perception that you aren't providing a superior level of customer service. All managers value customer service and pay attention to customer accusations. The external wound infects

COLLEAGUE BULLSHIT

your internal reputation.

Failing to convey legitimate customer concerns, withholding vital information, and using other tactics to make you look bad are techniques alliances formed against you will employ. By the time you learn of a problem, you're screwed because you weren't even aware there were issues. Your boss doesn't want to hear what really happened, because his focus is on solving the problem.

Why would a customer participate in an alliance against you? Customers have agendas too. Typically they want to get a product or service discounted or gratis. By placing one quick phone call, the plan is in motion and you are now being watched for giving substandard service. As this customer service problem escalates, your opposition jumps in and adds fuel to the fire. A simple statement such as, "Customer X says he never hears from him," becomes exaggerated internally to, "*No one* ever hears from him." The perception is in place, and you are now "a piece of shit who gives lousy customer service."

Alliances can also be formed when peers or members of management don't agree with your plan or strategy. They may come together in an effort to squelch it. Opportunists jump on board, perhaps by providing information to those who oppose you. Your plan is killed before it even gets started, and the opportunists have created allies they can call on for favors at a later time.

Let's face it, the more incompetent a person is, the less they want intelligent people around them. The quicker they can reduce this threat, the better. They insulate themselves by surrounding themselves with allies who don't threaten them or their way of life.

Your enemy can become your ally. Sometimes a simple favor is all it takes to convert them to your way of thinking, or to declare a truce. Corporate wars are in nobody's best interest. Valuable time and energy are wasted on activities that produce no profit. Watch carefully for alliances and be wary of participating in any of them. Diffusing a situation may be the best tactic of all.

TRUST

Trust no one

WHO CAN YOU TRUST in the corporate world? *No one.* Just as no one is out there to make you rich or get you promoted, no one comes to work in the morning to help you get ahead.

Everyone has an agenda. Beware of the person who spins a story that seems to slant in their favor and not yours. Are you being recruited to help them execute a plan? Are you about to become a cog in the wheel of their success? Watch out!

THE SUNSHINE PUMPER

"Hey, Boss, you're the best!"

EVERYONE LIKES AN EGO BOOST; it makes us feel *so* good. There are a lot of people out there who are very good at pumping sunshine up your ass to get what they want. Just remember, if they are pumping sunshine up *your* ass, they are probably doing the same with company executives or management.

If a fellow employee calls or talks to you several times a day to tell you what they are doing and how they are doing it, take heed. Continuously building value with you means they are doing the same thing with the boss. This is an agenda, and once they have convinced the boss of their worth, they'll keep chipping away until they get your job. You are really in trouble if your boss is an Egomaniac; she will be especially susceptible to this strategy.

The best protection you have is to stay in constant communication with management. Remind them of what value you bring to the company and why they hired you. Attend all meetings and communication sessions. Make sure that management knows who is doing the work. A Sunshine Pumper tries to create the perception that they are responsible for the success of everything. In reality, they are usually at the other end of the spectrum—they have put in very little effort.

Hold your cards close and be careful with whom you share your thoughts. The Sunshine Pumper always wants to be the one to share new ideas, especially if they can claim ownership of them.

One simple way to flush out a Sunshine Pumper is to tell a good joke. When a Sunshine Pumper hears it, they quickly go forth and spread it throughout the office. They take credit for the joke and create the perception that it is theirs. The more people they tell the joke to, the easier it is for them to create this perception.

Even though you can combat their activities, your ultimate goal should be to separate yourself from these people or get them out of your life altogether. Sunshine Pumpers consume a lot of your time; you'll spend days on end chasing your tail.

PATIENCE

Diabolical plans can take years to unfold

ADVERSARIES ARE PATIENT and are willing to put in an enormous amount of effort in order to advance their own agendas. Some people exert a lot of energy to achieve a small victory.

The patient person wins by their very nature. Either she is relentless and wears you down until you lose interest, or he demands so much of you that the end goal is no longer worth it to you. They win most of their battles by default because they have kept up a fight you gave up long ago.

Some battles rage on for years with no resolution. I once foiled a plan to overthrow the current management of my employer only to have the plan resurrect after I left the company two years later. They couldn't beat me so they just put their plans on hold until I was gone. If you find yourself in a similar situation, take a hard look at what you have to gain from a long battle and ask yourself, "Is this worth it?" If the answer is no, move on immediately. Don't waste one minute on this type of fight because the other side will never quit.

FORESIGHT

Learn to read the signs

WOULD YOU LIKE TO HAVE a crystal ball? Nobody can predict the future, but by using simple deductive reasoning, you may be able to determine what people are up to.

Observe the actions of the people around you and how they interact with others. Through personal experience, you probably have a good idea of what personality types are drawn to each other. Look for unusual relationships. Unexpected pairings may indicate that someone has a plan brewing. When you come across an unusual relationship, ask yourself what these people may have to gain by forming this alliance.

Physical mannerisms and mental attitudes can speak volumes as well. If you see two people roll their eyes in response to a comment, for example, they may well be plotting together. Their agenda may be to get an employee fired or to undermine you in some way. They may also begin to have cold or harsh attitudes toward anyone who stands in the way of their agenda. Their reactions will betray them, no matter how good a poker face they think they have.

Watch for strange decisions that come down from other departments. If you find yourself asking, "Why did they do that?" there is probably a reason, one that has something to do with advancing someone's personal agenda. Take a holistic view of the company. Looking at the big picture will help you interpret the signs. Analyze different scenarios and you will likely identify one that makes sense out of the seemingly senseless events and decisions that are swirling around you.

PERSUASION

Don't let them talk you into doing their work for them

"GET SOMEONE ELSE to do the dirty work" is a phrase that must have been born in the corporate environment. So if this saying is so damn familiar, why do we let ourselves get caught in this trap?

It's actually pretty easy to get caught. You may believe you are dealing with the "Good Guy," only to find out—too late—that Good Guy should have been named Backstabber.

Someone who can convince others to do the dirty work is often an opportunist. He or she looks for unrest within the company or among the employees. Anyone who is unhappy with their job, their boss, or who has recently been disciplined by someone in the company may become their accomplice.

A person in this frame of mind may be hell—bent on revenge. The opportunist takes advantage of this. Revenge is a very dangerous motivation and tends to make rational individuals do things they normally wouldn't even think of. Avengers are susceptible to suggestions and lies being told by an opportunist because the opportunist may be telling them exactly what they want to hear.

Your adversary will confide in their new accomplice and profess to have discovered a weak spot in you, one that makes you susceptible to attack. In reality there may be no such weak spot, but they have been successful in convincing the avenger to attack, thereby forcing you to defend yourself. Once you are on the defensive your adversary will undoubtedly recruit someone else to attack on another front. Pretty soon you'll be fighting on all fronts, with little effort put forth by your adversary. They have the time to focus on their job; you are doing anything but.

I have seen this tactic executed to an extreme degree by a company executive. This person was able to convince a former employee to file a lawsuit against a colleague in the company that he wanted to take out. Of course the person who filed the lawsuit had been fired and wanted revenge.

The lawsuit drained the resources of the defendant and managed to drag his good name through the mud as well. But the lawsuit served its purpose for the executive. The lawsuit had no merit, which didn't matter to him because he had nothing to gain from winning it anyway. His goal was simply to get someone else to fight his battle.

A strategy like this not only keeps the perpetrator clean but also creates a level of deniability. After all, why would a company executive encourage an ex-employee to sue the company? Wouldn't he also be hurting himself in the process? These are legitimate questions. On the surface, it seems the executive in question had very little at stake in the company. A losing lawsuit would have little effect on him personally, even though it would be devastating to the company.

But let's look at the motivation of this individual. He likely had an agenda. If this particular executive wanted to increase his equity stake in the company, it could have been to his advantage for the company to lose the suit. A loss would have had an adverse effect on the value of the company, or put the company out of business altogether. The executive could then buy in to the company at a discounted rate or purchase the company outright. Depending on the amount of damage that had been done, he could reopen the company under different management and become a hero, even though he was indirectly the one who drove the firm out of business. In this case the executive had everything to gain and nothing to lose by getting someone else to do his dirty work.

How might you prevent something like this happening to you? If you are a member of management, the best thing you can do is share the wealth a little. Make sure that your executives have something to lose if they head down this path. For everyone else, make sure that someone is not trying to convince you to do something that you shouldn't. No matter what has happened to you at your place of employment, don't let a need for revenge feed someone else's agenda.

THE RUMOR MILL

Keep your opponent busy on all fronts

SOME PEOPLE GET OTHERS to do their bidding; some fight their own battles. Whether fighting directly or indirectly, worthy adversaries keep their opponents focused on everything but their job and their own success. They know that one of the quickest ways to take out a competent rival is to make sure they are thoroughly distracted, to the point of not having enough hours in the day to complete their job.

If you find yourself fighting fires all day every day, stop and identify where they are coming from and who is setting them. You can bet that they are not being started by natural causes. Unfortunately, it's easier to start a fire than to extinguish one.

One effective fire-starter is the rumor mill. Rumors spread through a company like lightning. For example, a statement such as, "I heard Employee X is going to be fired," will by its very nature cause no end of headaches. First of all, the person who has made this statement didn't really say anything of substance. Therefore, they can plead ignorance if they are questioned about the statement later. All they did was start a rumor. In the meantime, the employee in question will undoubtedly hear the news and it will take several meetings to get the incident resolved. Your adversary has managed to make your life difficult with little or no effort on his part.

Rumors may be preceded by a land mine or two. For example, a coworker may say to you, "I heard Employee X was in the boss's office this morning. Do you know why he was called in?" Your colleague may have no idea why the two were talking, but he has managed to create the perception that the conversation was a bad one. Furthermore, he has encouraged another employee—you—to perpetuate the rumor by asking if you know any details.

How do you stop the rumor mill? For starters, confirm the substance of the news before you become an unsuspecting accomplice. If you have any doubt about what you have heard, speak directly with the source.

Most rumors die quickly when they are brought to light in a group setting. Tackle the gossip in a group meeting if possible, especially if all parties involved are present. You will see some serious backpedaling, and the person who backpedals the fastest is probably the one who started the rumors.

THE POINT SHAVER

"You owe me one"

WE ALL KNOW SOMEONE who is a Point Shaver. They keep score. Anything they do for you is recorded on their mental scoreboard, and they expect to be repaid at some point.

Points Shavers seem to remember what they have done for you, but forget what you have done for them. Whenever you ask them for a favor, they spew a long rendition of what they have done for you in the past, and how your new request will increase the debt you own them. They've forgotten how many times they cashed in on their favors.

The score is never tied with a Points Shaver. My advice is don't bother keeping score unless it's worth your time.

CONSPIRACIES

Let them hang themselves

SOMETIMES PEOPLE GET so tied up in executing their agendas, they self-destruct or burn themselves down in the process. As they get closer to their goal, they become so eager to tell someone of their impending victory that they prematurely reveal their plan, giving you ample opportunity to fight it.

Once they have let the cat out of the bag so to speak, they are vulnerable and any allies they have may begin to lose trust in them. Alliances are easily formed and easily broken. An overeager ally may jeopardize the grand plan and could be thrown under the bus by his co-conspirators. If the scheme unravels completely, he will become the scapegoat.

At some point, someone will likely get fired. If the plan involved overthrowing a superior, the target will identify those responsible and will remove them from the company. Or, the person who hatched the plan may lose his job because he is so caught up in his agenda that he is neglecting his work responsibilities.

Be patient and wait it out. Chances are good that conspirators won't be around for long.

GIVING CREDIT WHERE CREDIT IS DUE

Your adversary will take credit for a job well done whenever possible

I AM A FIRM BELIEVER in giving credit where credit is due. Unfortunately, not everyone shares my willingness to make others look good. Don't be surprised if others take credit for your work either directly or indirectly.

Here is what I mean. Taking credit directly is as simple as someone saying that the work you did was in fact completed by them. This of course is an outright lie. You won't see direct credit-taking that often, since it is fairly easy to disprove—especially if you've been taking my advice and been covering your ass.

The more common thing people do is take credit indirectly. Let's take the case of a common report, for example. Some people always want to be the person who takes the last look at a report to make sure it is done right. Once they have given the report their blessing they deliver the report to management. As they do so, they create the perception that they did the work, and they take the credit.

If the person who delivers the report to the boss happens to be your superior, you may hear them say, "I told the boss what a great job you're doing." Be worried. In reality they may be telling the boss what a great job *they* are doing and how they are mentoring you and fixing your mistakes. They may also be creating the perception that they have the best interest of the company in mind by bringing you along, thereby strengthening their position with the boss.

Minimize this by making sure you are part of the information delivery process. If some type of presentation is required, be part of it. Personally follow up with the powers-that-be to see if they have any questions about the work. They will then at least have an awareness of your involvement in the project.

CREATING PERCEPTIONS

Perception is reality

OUR PERCEPTIONS INFLUENCE our lives and affect most of the decisions we make. Some perceptions are self-evident: the grass is green and the sky is blue. Others perceptions may be influenced by people we value. Their perceptions may become our reality.

I am not talking about someone brainwashing you into believing something that isn't true. Rather, people sway our opinions about certain things or events and we *believe* them to be true. We see the power of perception every day. We make purchases, elect politicians, grant promotions, and even get married based on our beliefs about what a product does or who a person is.

Perceptions are created in the corporate environment by planting seeds. Someone makes a suggestion that is intended to lead you down a specific path. She drops hints such as, "I heard Employee X is getting fired." This simple statement creates an impression that Employee X is losing his job, even though that may be far from true. (See *Land Mines* and *Alliances*.)

Once the seed has been planted, it is followed up by a series of leading questions or statements in an effort to make the idea more credible. These questions are designed to help unsuspecting you convince yourself of the truth of some fact or event. Your perceptions become firmly planted in your mind because you have come to your own conclusion.

Here is an example from my life of how an opportunist took advantage of a simple spelling error and turned the error into a grave misperception. Our firm had two customers with company names that were pronounced the same but were spelled differently. (There was a one-letter difference.) In a presentation, the name of one of the companies was accidentally misspelled. The printed materials showed Company X's name, but the conversation was really about Company Y. The perpetrator saw this opportunity to discredit his coworker and decided to capitalize on it.

Our CEO was present in the meeting, but he was unaware that our firm had two customers whose names were so similar. Rather than correct the presenter in the meeting and clear up the spelling error, the perpetrator chose to speak with the CEO offline. He hinted that the presenter did not know his customers, as Company Y—the company that was the subject of the meeting—was in a completely different market than Company X, whose name was printed on the materials. He failed to mention that our firm served both companies. The perpetrator said to the CEO, "He doesn't know his customers well. Company Y is in a completely different industry. You may want to ask him what Company Y does."

The CEO did indeed ask the presenter about Company Y's business—or what he believed was Company Y. Of course the presenter began to talk about Company X. He updated the CEO on the wrong company!

This tiny seed of doubt helped the CEO convince himself of the presenter's lack of knowledge. Both parties were duped, all over a spelling error and selective transfer of information. It takes both a skilled manipulator and an ill-informed recipient to pull this off.

A skilled manipulator will also use this ability to buttress his worth within the organization. Statements such as, "The contract I'm working on could bring the company millions in revenue," imply future results. In reality none of these projects or business deals ever come to pass, but the manipulator has created the perception that he or she is invaluable to the company.

Why do people go to such effort to create false impressions? Usually it is to help advance a personal agenda, perhaps to receive a promotion, a raise, or the like. Often, the perpetrator hasn't convinced anyone that they have a better mousetrap; they have convinced them that they have mice and need a mousetrap.

TAKING THE WRONG PATH

Don't let anyone put your head in a noose

WE HAVE ALL HEARD the phrase "Give somebody enough rope and they will hang themselves." Unfortunately, this doesn't happen that often. Usually, someone puts a noose around their neck.

Sometimes you're the target. How does this work? Typically, the person who wants to see you hang uses various tactics to get you headed down the wrong path.

Perhaps at one time they made a suggestion to management about a particular idea or project. Their idea was rejected, so your nemesis knows the initiative is something the company is opposed to. They set their plan in motion by convincing you to pursue the worthless idea, claiming that the rejected project is something that would greatly benefit the company and your career as well.

Misdirection can only succeed if your adversary can somehow prevent you from having any discussions with management about the project. Otherwise, management will get wind of your efforts and will redirect you. To keep you isolated, your executioner stresses that the project is confidential, and you should not discuss it with anyone. This enables them to keep you moving on the project without anyone getting wise to their plan. Before long you will be knee—deep in a bogus project or idea and may very well be beyond the point of recovery. When it comes time to present the idea to management, your enemy will encourage you to present it yourself saying, "It's your work and doing this will be good for your career." In reality, they are distancing themselves from you and the project so they have deniability when you present the doomed idea.

Your defense against this type of diabolical plan is simple. Keep everyone in the loop, including management. It's up to you to make them aware of what you are working on and with whom you are working. If the schemer balks at the suggestion of including everyone who might have an interest in the project, be careful. They may not have your best interest in mind.

THE OFFICE FLIRT

"I think we all know what this is by now"

DON'T GET INVOLVED. Nothing good can come from it. Don't even think about it!

LAND MINES

Walk carefully

ADVERSARIES ARE PATIENT. They may lay a series of land mines for you, hoping that you step on one or all of them. Land mines are convincing, effective ways to exploit the power of suggestion. Here is how they work.

The person who plants a land mine wants to create a perception about a person or an idea. They know full well that merely telling you juicy information about someone won't make you believe it. You will likely dismiss the idea as hearsay or gossip. In order to get you to believe their land mine, they need cooperation from the person they are talking about. For example, someone might say, "I heard So-and-So is having marital problems." This statement is now nestled in the back of your mind. The next time you speak with the person who is supposedly having marital problems, they mention that they had a disagreement with their spouse. Even though the truth is that the couple has a great relationship and they just had a minor spat as most people do, you perceive that they are having marital problems based on the statement that you heard earlier. You have just fallen victim to a land mine.

The objective of a land mine is to get you to work against yourself. Your adversary may have been planting negative suggestions in your manager's head for weeks, just waiting for you to make a small mistake.

One mistake is not the end of the world, but the effect is much greater if the power of suggestion works against you. If management becomes upset about things that seem insignificant then someone may be laying land mines in your path.

Always verify any information that someone says about another person. Make sure you communicate with those around you, especially management. They need to hear from you on a regular basis so they are less likely to believe negative statements about you. Taking a few precautions will help keep land mines from exploding in your face.

FRIENDS AND ENEMIES

Friends may not be friends

FRIEND OR FOE? I find myself asking this question more and more. In the corporate world, it is sometimes difficult to tell the difference between someone who is your friend and someone who is merely posing as one.

A foe posing as a friend is likely doing so just to gather information. With foes, information typically flows only one way—toward them. You won't see much information coming from them. They will hoard data, or they may intentionally withhold it from you. Foes also like to target phone and e-mail messages. They may conveniently "forget" to give you that message you were expecting or forward an e-mail that contains information critical to your project.

Withholding information enables the foe to create an adverse case against you behind the scenes. They build up evidence of your incompetence as things go wrong or don't get done. In reality the problems that are occurring are problems you don't even know about.

If you think something strange is going on, you can protect yourself. First, make sure no one but you is responsible for your phone messages. You may even have to forward your office calls to your home or mobile number if you are frequently out of the office.

If your job includes presenting plans or projects to management,

COLLEAGUE BULLSHIT

make sure you are the one doing the presentation whenever possible. At least attend the meeting. Never let anyone present your ideas in your absence.

Be savvy and watch for evidence of backdoor communication. If you receive an e-mail reply from someone who was not copied on an original e-mail, they were probably blind copied without your knowledge. This is a common tool used by a foe. Always assume that anyone could receive any e-mail you send. And assume that those who control flow of information to you are probably doing the same to others.

CHANGED ATTITUDES

Learn to read signals

THE QUICKEST WAY FOR ME to tell if someone is up to something is a change in his attitude. If a person becomes colder toward you but suddenly warms to another or vice versa, it may mean they have identified a new path to advance their own agenda.

The phrase "Politics makes strange bedfellows" is never more evident than here. A person may create an alliance with someone he previously disliked or discredited because that person promised him something or he identified an opportunity that furthers each of their agendas. You never know what deals people have made to advance in the organization or to keep themselves in good standing with the company.

Pay special attention if you see this type of attitude change in a subordinate. If you are their manager and their demeanor changes rapidly, you may no longer hold any value for them. They may even become incorrigible. If a subordinate needs you to advance their agenda, their newfound devotion to you will be equally obvious.

This type of behavior may warn you of impending changes in the company. If a person turns cold to you, it may mean that they have been in to see your boss and learned that you will no longer be managing them or may even no longer be working there. Similarly, if a person who was previously dismissive of you warms to you, that usually means they have judged that the relationship between you and your boss is strong, and they may need to figure out a way to stay on your good side.

INFORMATION

Check your sources

INFORMATION IS LIKELY the most valuable commodity in the business world. It can help you advance your career and make more money. Never forget that people transfer information. As the transfer occurs, accuracy is lost exponentially. Inaccurate information has no value.

Confirm all information at its source to confirm its validity. Don't believe it because you want it to be true. Don't make decisions based on gossip. Be careful of any data that comes from the town crier. It is unlikely that this person has accurate info. They are likely just spreading rumors. And if they are spreading rumors about someone else to you, they are likely telling tales about you to someone else. For some reason, town criers get an ego boost by making themselves appear smarter or "in the know."

Multimillion-dollar industries have been built on the premise that information can be wrong. If you have ever seen an advertisement to purchase a copy of your credit report, then you know what I am talking about. We pay to make sure that the data someone gathers about us is accurate. We know that just because "it's in the system" doesn't make it true.

THE NETWORKER

"I have a friend..."

I'M SURE YOU RECOGNIZE the Networker—the person who spends more time networking than working. They believe that the road to success is about whom you know, not what you know.

I have watched people do nothing but network all day long. One guy worked from 8:00 a.m. to 10:00 p.m. almost every day. Initially I thought he was a very hard worker. One afternoon a few of his coworkers showed up at happy hour and I asked them why he worked so much. It turns out that he was spending the entire day walking around the office, bullshitting with everyone and then doing his work after hours.

Don't get sucked into the web of a Networker. They name-drop and appear to be connected. In reality they are just bullshitters. They burn up a lot of your valuable time with meaningless office chitchat. It doesn't take long for everyone to get tired of them. Hanging around them won't add much to your value.

NETWORKING

Know those who are truly well-connected

NETWORKERS CLAIM TO BE CONNECTED within the company. There are also those who claim connections outside of the company. Ask yourself, "Is this true, or are they just bullshitting me?"

I have run across a lot of people during my career who claim to be connected and seem to know everybody. They are telling the truth, but those they know have no value. They may be able to get you a free beer at the local pub but not much at all in the corporate world.

If you do find a person with connections who can get things done for you, make sure the favor is worth the price. Someone like that almost always wants something in return. Don't ask if you can't afford it.

REVENGE

Sticking it to someone usually backfires

DURING YOUR CAREER you will undoubtedly come across someone who feels they have been wronged, who is hell—bent on revenge. Revenge is a dangerous motivation and can make people do things they wouldn't normally do. If you have ever heard stories of an ex-husband or ex-wife chain-sawing the house in half after a nasty divorce, then you know what we are dealing with here.

Revenge is a common motivation for Egomaniacs. If you or someone else has bruised their ego, they may harbor their anger for years, and you might think everything is fine. Then one day out of nowhere, the attacker strikes.

Some seek payback directly and avenge you themselves. Part of their satisfaction is witnessing your pain. Others do it indirectly and use others to inflict their damage. (See *Persuasion.*) This enables them to disguise their plan and attack you on multiple fronts.

Direct revenge is fairly easy to deal with because you know where it is coming from. You can deal with that person one on one. You typically know your attacker because they *want* you to know. Since the damage is so obvious, they are likely to face consequences they did not think about while exacting their revenge. I liken this scenario to a liquor store robber whose crime is caught on the video security camera. The perpetrator is identified and they go to jail.

Indirect revenge is more dangerous. It usually unfolds over a long period of time and is likely to be executed through individuals we would never suspect. This enables the avenger to "have their day," yet stay free of any consequences.

The person who seeks indirect revenge is often an opportunist. They wait patiently and recruit accomplices along the way. As they listen to idle chitchat around the office they find people who don't agree with your views or who have had small disagreements with you. They then recruit by befriending the offended party—perhaps over a long period of time— talking with them, fueling the fire, and turning small issues into big ones. This unknowing accomplice may become agitated and more and more a thorn in your side. Multiple accomplices like these can make your life hell, thus exacting your enemy's sweet revenge. The perpetrator comes out clean and has put forth very little effort.

Plots like these seem to unfold in passive-aggressive ways. They create frustrating situations that spark negative reactions in you. Be careful—strong backlash on your part makes you look like the bad guy, which is just what the perpetrator wants. So don't overreact. Assess the situation as a whole and try to remove accomplices from the mix. This will help you determine who is behind the attack.

Once you have identified the perpetrator, determine how far that person is willing to go to seek revenge. Some people are like suicide bombers; if they are willing to die for the cause there is little you can do to defend yourself. In such cases, you must evaluate what their end goal is and try to head them off. The best way to do this is to disclose to the unwitting accomplices what their role has been in the plan. Sometimes they back off once they understand that they've been duped.

SAFE COMMUNICATION

Someone is always watching, listening, or reading

THESE DAYS CORPORATE communication modes are highly scrutinized, much like security at a casino. Someone is always watching. Virtually all information flows through a computer at some point, which enables other people to access what you are doing. I don't have a problem with companies monitoring employee activity. But a problem arises when information is shared with those who shouldn't have access to it.

If someone is after your job, for example, every e-mail you send may be monitored by their buddy in the IT department. This gives them an advantage and allows them to always be a step ahead of you. They can steal your ideas and create the perception that they are the better person for the job.

You can't not communicate; just be careful how you do it. If you have a conversation that must remain confidential, talk with your colleague one-on-one or take the meeting offsite to avoid prying eyes and ears. If you must communicate on company channels, be careful to whom you send information and don't copy a lot of people on e-mails. You don't know where that data will wind up or to whom it will get forwarded without your knowledge or approval.

In general, don't share anything across corporate channels you wouldn't want everyone to see because they just might!

BLAME

Don't be the fall guy

WHEN PEOPLE SET OUT to perform a task or project, there are two possibilities: success or failure. Some people develop a strategy for either outcome so they can take credit for success and blame someone else for failure. They lay their groundwork early in the process.

This is how it's done. The perpetrator may make a simple off-the-cuff remark about your ability to make the project a success. These remarks may continue through the course of the project to reinforce doubts about you. Unfortunately for you they are always off the record and never spoken while you are around. These comments won't be remembered unless someone needs to recall them in order to assign blame. The perpetrator is using the power of suggestion against you. They have established an opportunity to assign blame to you if the project fails just by saying, "I told you so."

If the project is a success, the off-the-record remarks will be forgotten and the perpetrator will take credit for all of your effort.

There are some steps you can take to make sure that you don't become the fall guy for a failed project. For starters, take an objective view of it and ask yourself if it can succeed. Is there enough time available to get it done? If you believe there is, then document milestones and responsibilities. A well-documented project plan is your ally. It is more difficult for someone to assign blame or take credit if there is clear evidence supporting your role. Keep the "powers that be" informed on the project progress. Do this yourself or at least be present when the updates take place. This will allow you to get exposure to management and squash any doubts about your ability.

THE TEN-CENT MILLIONAIRE

"I've got money in the bank"

THROUGHOUT YOUR CAREER, you will encounter people of varying wealth and status. I've found this dynamic to be true: It seems that those who really have money try to create the perception that they do not. In contrast, the people who don't have money try to create the perception that they do.

The Ten-Cent Millionaire usually falls into the category of those who have not rather than those who have. Status is very important to them and they go to great lengths to perpetuate an illusion of wealth. Typically they are leveraged to the hilt and banks or mortgage companies own everything they have.

Ten-Cent Millionaires try to draw you into their inner circle. They do this by claiming that you can be rich like them if you help them out. Don't fall for this tactic. Those who are true millionaires have found a way to make a lot of money and won't likely invite you to share their wealth. You will have to earn their secrets to success.

SHARING WEALTH

Everyone wants a piece of the pie

PEOPLE ARE MORE LIKELY to be team players if they have a stake in the game. You can either share the success with others who have helped make it happen, or watch them try to take it from you.

If people are looking for their due, they'll figure out a way to get it. They will engage in political undermining and maneuvering that is second to none and may even lead to failure of the company. Those who have been slighted may intentionally create unrest or drive the company into the ground. If they drive the value of the company down, they can buy it cheap, essentially stealing the organization's intellectual property for personal gain.

People need to be rewarded for their hard work. Make sure you know what is waiting for you at the finish line. Don't assume there is going to be a gold medal if you win. You may get nothing more than a pat on the back and an entry form for the next race.

BIG PLANS

Be wary of promises

MOST OF US HAVE WORKED with the person who has big plans. We hear them say things like, "In a year I'll be running this place," or, "Someday I'll own this company." Statements like these are usually more recruiting technique than reality.

In most cases these people are reaching out, looking for people to help them execute their agenda. They may promise you wealth and power under their new management and tell you there will be a place for you in the company once they have taken it over. Don't fall for this crap. Once you've helped them get to where they want to be, you will become expendable and likely get nothing for your efforts.

If you decide to take a risk with them, get their promises in writing. This is important, because you will be working with them against the goals of current management. This won't put you in a very good light if the plan fails. Also, the people who hatch these plans usually establish a scapegoat to take the blame if the plan goes awry. You may very well be the person they've chosen, so be careful.

RELATIONSHIPS

People do what they want to do

DURING YOUR CAREER you will have to deal with individuals who may hear you but don't listen to you. Some people have all the answers and would rather tell you about them than listen to your opinions. This is frustrating no matter what, but it is particularly so if you are working with a person who has less experience than you.

People like this are very similar to a child in a kitchen. No matter how many times you tell the kid that the pan is hot, she won't believe you until she has burned herself. It is equally painful for you to watch employees learn via trial and error rather than listen to the voice of experience. It is not only time consuming, it is also costly for the company. Eventually they will wind up on the path that you recommended in the beginning but by then it will be their idea and not yours.

When you come across people like this, there are few options. Since they don't listen to you and refuse to learn from your experience, remove yourself from the situation. To them, you have no real value. They are going to do it their way regardless of any advice you've given them. By stepping back early, you'll be less likely to be in their line of fire when they try to make you accountable for their failures.

SET-UPS

It doesn't feel good to be framed

MOST OF US CAN SEE a set-up coming a mile away. You know when someone seeks personal advancement or when he feels wronged for whatever reason and wants revenge. If a person views you as an obstacle in his path, he may set you up to get back at you or to get his way.

A set-up is nothing more than a frame job—a feeble attempt to let you take the fall for some event that may have damaged the employee or the company. Most of these are premeditated, but the plan is usually not well-orchestrated and therefore fails before it even gets started.

There is, however, a dangerous set-up plan that can catch you by surprise. Almost every organization has an opportunist, a person we might call a snake in the grass. An opportunist gathers information that may have little value to them but great value to someone else. When the opportunist hears a piece of information, they evaluate it and determine who in the organization may benefit from it the most. They may then go to that person and see if they can barter a service or form an alliance. In the case of an alliance, the opportunist achieves advancement or gains some other favorable recognition within the organization.

Be careful with whom you share information; be aware who is present when you discuss business. The opportunist is always lurking and may share whatever you have to say without your knowledge. You may never know who "set you up" until it is too late.

Most of this information is mined in the bar after hours. If you are going to go out after work, choose your company carefully. In most cases you are better off going out with your non—work friends and leaving your coworkers behind.

THE GODFATHER

"I run the show"

THE GODFATHER ENJOYS reminding everyone—coworkers and clients alike—that he is in charge. He takes any opening in a conversation to mention that the world works for him and that *he* will make sure people are doing what they've been told to do.

The Godfather typically doesn't fix problems, even if the issue at hand is his responsibility to correct. Instead, he informs you that he has assigned someone to fix the problem.

Even if you don't work for the Godfather and aren't associated with his company, he will still imply that he has some control over you. If you have ever heard someone say, "I know your boss," or, "I have a direct line to your boss," you are dealing with the Godfather. In most cases, Godfather-types are full of hot air and aren't as influential as they think they are. The best thing to do when you encounter him is to let him think he is in charge, then go about your business as usual.

LIES

There are liars, and then there are liars

LIES WITHIN AN ORGANIZATION are perpetrated at several different levels. Most people rarely lie, and when they do so, they don't do it intentionally. They may justify their lies because they have to protect the company in some way. More often than not, a person will withhold information from you or redirect questions to keep from lying. They want no part of it.

Some people, however, are chronic liars. The chronic liar is very believable. They succeed because they help you convince yourself that some piece of false information is true. They create perceptions over time about something they want you to believe.

I once encountered a chronic liar who had it in for another employee. As an opportunist he noticed when his "enemy" left for doctor appointments and offsite meetings. The liar strategically commented to his enemy's boss that, "He is always leaving early," and left it at that. With every offsite meeting his enemy attended, the opportunist would repeat, "He is always leaving early." Eventually, the enemy was disciplined for leaving early, all because of the opportunist's lies.

Don't get caught up with a chronic liar. Verify any information you are given about people. You may have to formulate your questions carefully in order to get the verification you need. Ask pointed questions and stick to the facts.

Liars eventually get exposed because they have told so many lies that they no longer know the truth. Unfortunately, their exposure only happens with time, and they may have caused untold damage before their true character is revealed.

GIFTS

Keep up your guard

AS THE OLD SLOGAN GOES "You don't get something for nothing." When people help you or are generous toward you in the workplace, their kindness usually comes with a price.

These days I am more suspicious of the person helping me than I am of the one who is trying to trip me up. I expect corporate politics. I recognize the signs and can formulate a defense against my adversaries' plans. But I don't expect gifts of kindness to be used against me or for someone else's gain.

I am most suspicious of the person who says, "I told the boss you are doing a great job." This one has come back to bite me before. I earned praise for my hard work. My boss even bought me a gift as a reward for my efforts. But he took all the credit. I came to view that present as a congratulatory gift he gave himself, to pat himself on the back for sticking it to me. Be wary of overt generosity.

CORPORATE LADDER

The ladder is crowded

MOST PEOPLE WANT to move up the ladder and advance their career. Let's face it: We could all use a little more income along the way. Just remember, if you're climbing the ladder, you aren't the only one on it.

Some people will think nothing of leaving a trail of bodies on each rung. If someone is trying to make a move up, take note of where you fit in to the picture. If you are in a lower position than the person making their advance, you won't have much value to them, and they will barely have the time of day for you. If you are in an equal position to them, they may ask for your help in their quest for the top. If you are above them, they will suck up to you in order to gain your trust because they need your help to advance. Your job may be their next target.

If you keep this natural progression in mind, you will be able to tell who is on the advance just by their attitude toward you. Be careful with whom you share information, especially if a person seems overly interested in your day-to-day activities. This information will likely be used against you at a later date. Very rarely does someone else benefit from sending their boss or anyone else to the top. Sooner or later someone will step on your fingers and try to knock you off the ladder.

TIMING

Quarterly goals are no secret

"WE MUST MEET our quarterly goals," they say. Fine. Trouble is, these company goals are likely out of line with our customers' goals. I promise you, your customers have no intention of giving your company a revenue boost.

All too often the company forces its revenue goals on its customers. Neither company nor customer benefit from this short-term solution.

Pronouncements from on high sometimes backfire. A short-term solution becomes long-term sacrifice. For example, our customers know that we push to close business at the end of every quarter. Knowing our hunger to meet management's expectations, they patiently wait until the end of the quarter to buy. They achieve their goals of getting the best possible price because they know our company is more likely to discount at that time. We may have met our short-term targets, but we have cost ourselves long-term revenue. Why? We've turned control of our pricing over to our customers.

Customers take a risk by doing this. Project timelines may be changed or costly delays may occur because they wait to make their purchase. Often, this is a trade-off customers are willing to make.

We can maintain a healthier and more profitable relationship with our customers by keeping our goals in sync with theirs as we interact with them on a daily basis. Learn to think long-term and your customer relationships will significantly improve. Customers might even start taking your phone calls if they know you keep their interests in mind.

THE REPAIRMAN

"I'll fix it"

THE REPAIRMAN IS AN INTERESTING personality. Typically very bright and a tremendous problem solver, the Repairman enjoys coming to the rescue. He comes up with creative solutions and everyone pats him on the back to congratulate his ingenuity.

If you are a proactive person, the Repairman will frustrate you to no end. He prefers to wait for a problem to occur, then he fixes the symptoms. He doesn't seem to recognize that preventing a problem is more effective than fixing one. Sometimes I've even seen Repairmen cause a problem so they can have the joy of solving it.

Repairmen's hearts are in the right place, but problem solving isn't as helpful as problem prevention. Do your best to help them see the benefits of prevention. Document any problems you anticipate and take notes on any discussions you have with the Repairman about it. (He will likely be resistant to prevention.) When the problem occurs, discuss it with him, and show him how much time could have been saved by not having the problem occur at all. Once you have proven your point a couple of times, he may become a convert and start reciting Ben Franklin's phrase "An ounce of prevention is worth a pound of cure."

TIME THEFT

Limit the number of hoops you're willing to jump through

IF YOU WORK DIRECTLY with customers, you are undoubtedly strapped for time. What time you have can easily be consumed by a few clients who think you are the answer to their problems. Don't be your own worst enemy. Great customer service is important, but it's okay to encourage your customer to be a little more self-sufficient.

Don't set unrealistic expectations of what you can offer. This is especially true with prospective or new customers. First, determine if the person you are working with has any intention of buying. Keep in mind that the customer relationship is a two-way street; the customer should be willing to make some commitment to you in exchange for the service you provide them. When working with a prospective or new customer, find out what tasks they require you to complete. Once these are clear, get a commitment from them, that they will complete an event once you meet their requirements. The event may be execution of a contract, purchase of additional goods, or something as simple as paying their invoice once their problem is solved.

Put a value on your time and make sure the customer respects that value. If the customer insists on abusing your time, require them to pay for your expertise once their demands exceed the basic service you normally deliver. If your customer is serious about the business relationship, they won't refuse you.

Beware of companies that call you looking for bids or dangling promises of large lucrative contracts. They likely want one of two things: a competitive price in order to keep their current supplier honest, or free consulting services at your expense.

You may have to have a difficult conversation with a prospective customer. I once had to say, "Even if I had a million dollars of your business, I would go out of business." After this conversation, their time-consuming calls stopped and I was free to spend my time more profitably. Don't be afraid to demand value for your time and secure some kind of commitment before you give your time away.

INDUSTRY RELATIONSHIPS

Call in favors when you need to

INDUSTRY RELATIONSHIPS are invaluable and can save you if you get in a jam. Constantly cultivate them and guard them carefully because they may be used against you. Nothing gets the attention of management like a dissatisfied major customer.

If a rival can't beat you within the company, he may try to beat you externally. The easiest way for him to do so is to convince a strategic customer to complain about you.

If you have diligently stayed in contact with customers and maintained your industry relationships, no one will be able to bullshit them and cut you out of the loop. Your cultivation of these valuable relationships may help you in times of need. Bad news from a customer can hurt you, but good news from a customer can also save you.

YOUR OWN
BULLSHIT

MAKING MONEY

Focus on what makes money

CORPORATIONS ARE IN the business of making money, and you should be too. Think of yourself as a profit center for You, Inc. If you focus on the things that will make you successful, both you and your employer will reap the rewards of your efforts.

The most valuable commodity you have is your own time. Spend it wisely. For example, don't invest eight hours putting together a presentation when you can deliver the same results with only an hour's prep time. Management wants the content of your message, not a bunch of fluff and pretty artwork. Countless times, I have seen a presenter cut short and their ideas not even considered because the managers ran out of time before she got to the meat of her idea.

I am all for the concept of *team,* but beware of committees that get out of hand and waste everyone's time. If you must send your idea to committee, set specific goals and keep things on track. Timelines and deadlines are crucial for a group decision-making environment to succeed. Assign tasks to individuals; hold them accountable for results. Are the tasks you've assigned within their competencies? Are they within yours? If you manage this process properly, you can take advantage of the skills others bring to the table without having to do everything yourself.

Define your core competency and stick with it. If you try to do everyone else's jobs, you won't be able to do your own. You, Inc. will suffer.

CORPORATE DIRECTION

Default to what's best for the company

IF YOU ALIGN YOUR GOALS with the goals of the company, your life will be much easier. Remember, the company is there for the company—not for you. If you can't decide what direction to take or figure out where the company is headed, ask one simple question: "What's best for the company in this situation?" You will likely get your answer.

Companies change and you must change with them. Keep an open mind and don't be afraid of this. Be flexible when it comes to your career path, even if it means changing careers midstream. Some of the most successful people I know are following a much different career path now than they set out to in the beginning. Be prepared for change and stay ahead of the curve. If you can anticipate where the company is headed and can help lead them there, you will be miles ahead of your counterparts who may be fighting the change.

Flexibility in your career may take you a long way, especially in tough economic times. You will be decidedly more likely to keep your job if you can demonstrate a willingness to change. Following a new product line or moving to a new division of the company may very well be a good career move. It could also put a few more dollars in your pocket.

Don't be too arrogant when it comes to assessing the value you provide for the company. Few organizations bank their success or failure on one individual. Everyone is expendable and don't think for one minute that the company can't survive without you. This is a very dangerous mindset and you'll end up blindsided by the inevitable corporate restructuring.

PERSONAL INVESTING

Investment advisors get paid with your money

Front—loading, back—loading, A shares, B shares, no—load funds, loaded funds. If all of this sounds Greek to you, you are not alone. The more confused you become with all of these investment options, the more likely you are to seek the advice of an investment professional. This is exactly what this convoluted system is designed to do.

I am not recommending that you do your own investing, but there are some things to keep in mind when you head down the investment advisor path. First, investment advisors get paid with *your* money. If you purchase one of their offerings, some portion of *your* money goes into *their* pocket. How much depends on what product they sell you.

Advisors tend to steer you away from options that don't pay them well. It's almost like you should buy whatever they least want to sell you. The best product for you is probably the lowest moneymaker for them. Do your best to educate yourself on all of the options available to you. Ask a lot of questions. If you are still unsure, don't invest *anything* until you understand the investment fully.

Advisors sometimes receive bonuses when they sell a particular fund or investment product. They get the bonuses whether or not the product is what you truly need.

I never deal with an investment professional who isn't willing to share his own portfolio with me. During your initial interview, ask them directly: "What are you invested in personally? What's in your portfolio?" Although their personal investments may not be right for you, their willingness to be open will be an indication of their honesty and interest in genuinely helping you.

PROMOTIONS AND RAISES

Ask and you will receive

EVERYONE WANTS THE BIG promotion, and the extra money that goes with it. The promotion or advancement usually goes to the person who asks for it and wants it the most. On more than a few occasions, I have had someone enter my office after a promotion has been awarded, confused about why they didn't receive it. In a few cases, the individual had not asked to be considered for the position. So guess what? They weren't!

Be clear. Management needs to understand your personal and professional goals and accomplishments. Set expectations according to these goals and communicate them. Give realistic timelines and tell management what you want to be paid or what you envision yourself doing at certain points in your career. It is unlikely that you'll receive what you don't request. So speak up!

MR. NEGATIVE

"The thing is..."

HOW MANY TIMES HAVE YOU said something positive only to have Mr. Negative come back and cut you right down? He can find the negative side to anything. Mr. Negative could win $100 million playing the lottery and still bitch because it wasn't $200 million.

Mr. Negative isn't hard to find. Just ask him a question and see if he comes back with a negative spin. Key phrases like, "The thing about it is," "The problem is," or "I don't think that will work," quickly identify this character. A simple word of advice for dealing with Mr. Negative: stay the hell away from him; keep him out of your life. All he does is spread doom and gloom and create negative attitudes in everyone else.

TITLES

The title should be the real thing

TITLES IN THE BUSINESS world carry status and help us take pride in our accomplishments. They also provide us with a sense of where we have been and where we are going. Sometimes they command respect. Sometimes they inspire awe. The question is, Are they worth it?

A bigger title usually comes with a pay raise and more perks. Some companies have discovered that a simple change in title with few additional incentives is enough to keep a person motivated. This doesn't make sense to me at all. If you are going to take on more responsibility, put in more time, and add more value to the company, there should be something substantial in it for you. Take time to fully evaluate any promotion. Doing more work for the same pay or less seems like a demotion—not a promotion—to me.

NEGOTIATION

You won't get more than you ask for

WHEN WE NEGOTIATE, we try to get the most *we* can from someone who is trying to get the most *they* can. Sometimes it gets a little sticky. That's fine. Don't be afraid to negotiate.

In your beginning conversation, ask for more than you expect to get. This will help you understand the playing field and it will give you an idea of where you stand. On the rare occasion that you get what you ask for the first time, you may be amazed that you achieved a better result than you expected. You may also wonder, "Could I have gotten more?" So start high. You may not get what you ask for, but you won't leave anything on the table either.

Don't be afraid to walk away from the deal. Most people don't negotiate well because they really want what the other person has and they don't want to risk losing it. Whether it's a big contract, a job, a promotion, or a new car, be willing to walk away. You will be pleasantly surprised at how much better your negotiations turn out. Suddenly, what you offer carries value, and the tables often turn.

Finally, research your adversary. Find out what motivates her. Use this information to determine what you may need to do to "sweeten the pot." Knowing your counterpart's preferences prevents you from needlessly conceding on items she doesn't care about. She may not desire what you "throw in," but she certainly won't refuse it if you're willing to give it up.

SUCCESS

Know how you define success

CAREER SUCCESS IS one of the crowning achievements of our lives. We all want to attain it, but what exactly is *it*? Are we striving to meet our own definition of success, or are we chasing someone else's dream?

Take time to consider how you define success. Your definition may be different from someone else's, and what is great for you may not be important to them. Once you have decided how you want to measure your success, set goals. Make them realistic, but don't set them too low. Most of us are capable of achieving a lot more than we give ourselves credit for. Think of when you were a kid learning to ride a bike. Since you didn't know how to ride, you probably felt most comfortable on a small model. Once you learned how to ride, you outgrew the small bike very quickly and wanted a bigger one. Career goals are a lot like learning to ride a bike. When you go into the unknown, you tend to set your goals lower than they should be. So get the bigger bike. You may get a few bumps and bruises along the way, but you will master it sooner than you think.

Once you are successful, others will want to follow. I call this success by association. Be very careful with whom you share your success, and your secrets to attaining it. People who follow success are like hyenas on the Serengeti. They don't care who killed the gazelle; they just want their piece of the kill.

Protect the intellectual property of You, Inc. Don't share it with someone unless there is something in it for you; otherwise you are just creating competition for yourself.

THOSE IN CHARGE

Study the leaders

IT'S WISE PRACTICE to evaluate who is leading the company you work for, or might potentially work for. I've listed below some questions to ask when you are considering a career change.

How did the leaders rise to their positions? Did they work their way up from within, or were they hired from outside the company?

Is this their first leadership role or do they have several years of experience?

Do they know the industry well? (After all, what works in one industry may not work in another.)

What other qualities do they exhibit as a leader?

What is their vision for the company?

Take time to create some questions of your own. You may value other aspects of leadership that aren't represented in this list. How you answer these questions can help you determine whether to stay with your current company or move on.

THE EGOMANIAC

"I need to feel good about myself"

OUR EGOS DRIVE all of us. Everyone likes to feel important and needed. Some people—I call them Egomaniacs—take this to the extreme, almost to the point of addiction.

Egomaniacs are easy to spot throughout your organization. They seek the limelight every chance they get. Attention of any kind is hard for them to resist. They have an insatiable urge to take credit for everything that goes well and immediately assign blame for anything that goes poorly. They admit no mistakes and have an explanation for everything. They are big on job titles and perks. The impressive job titles not only give them the respect Egomaniacs think they deserve, but they also reinforce Egomaniacs' perceptions that they have something others don't.

Be careful when you deal with an Egomaniac. For one thing, he will do almost anything to feed his "addiction," and will go to great effort to protect his sources of supply. Other people may do things for his benefit—even things that may go against their better judgment—either because he has manipulated them into doing so, or because they recognize his addiction and want to use his weakness to their advantage. If you get between an Egomaniac and his "dealer," you're the one likely to get hurt. An Egomanic's ego is actually quite fragile, and if it gets bruised, he is more likely to do anything he can to harm you than to recall the thousand compliments you've given him through the years.

Having an Egomaniac in a high-level position is counterproductive. The decisions he makes are rarely in the best interest of the company or his fellow employees. He is most likely to make a choice that betters his position or further feeds his addiction in some way.

Most Egomaniacs have an Achilles' heel you can easily exploit. In the process of inflating their own egos, they almost always make a lot of promises in order to create the perception that they are persons who get things done. At the end of the day, these promises are bullshit and there is no way they can deliver on all of them. In other words, they talk big but don't accomplish anything.

Like the Politician, documentation is an Egomaniac's enemy. Be discrete but document everything they promise. Over time, the large gap between what they have promised and what they actually deliver will be evident, and you will be able to expose them. Before you take this step, be sure you can present a solid case. Your confrontation will be a huge blow to their ego and they will do everything they can to keep anyone from questioning their self-image.

COVERING EXPENSES

Let the company foot the bill

YOUR COMPENSATION arrangement with your employer will have to handle in some way the inevitable business expenses. In most cases, it is to your advantage to have your employer pay these, not you.

Expense liability can be an infinite risk. If you agree to cover expenses, those expenses may far outweigh any financial benefit you receive from your employer or employment contract. Beware: Some businesses aren't profitable if an employer has to shoulder all expenses. They can only be profitable if the employer can convince you to pay them.

If you bear the operating expenses yourself, you may be able to deduct those items from your personal or company income tax. But that's not always a wise approach. If you take a tax deduction, you will likely not be fully reimbursed for the expenditure. For example, if you are in a thirty percent tax bracket, a $100 expenditure will only reduce your tax liability by $30. You are still out of pocket $70. If your employer reimburses you for the expense, you will likely receive the full $100 reimbursement for the $100 expenditure, leaving you with no out-of-pocket loss.

If you work under employer reimbursement, spend the company's money wisely. If you treat the company's money like it is your own, you will probably never lock horns with the accounting department.

Make sure all expenditures produce value that will benefit the company. When you entertain potential customers or clients, evaluate which ones are serious about doing business with you, and which ones only want a free lunch. Unnecessary lunch and dinner meetings are not only a drain on the company, but can cost you valuable time you could be investing with customers who want to do business with you.

ADDING VALUE

You are expendable

COMPANIES ARE IN THE BUSINESS of making money. To a certain extent, we all have to pull the company line and help keep the revenue machine running.

Make sure that you continually add value to the company. Find ways to improve yourself and your processes. All employees are expendable and if it makes financial sense to the company, you will be replaced or eliminated altogether.

YOUR FUTURE

You take care of you

AT SOME POINT in your career, you've probably been told that you have a bright future in the company and will go far. Of course you like to feel vital to the success of the company and comfortable that you have a solid future. The key is to make sure that you *have* a future and you're not just being led to believe that you do.

Own your destiny. No one is out to make you rich or take care of you. Your career path should be clear-cut and tied to your achievements. Milestones should be accompanied by personal rewards. Make it very simple: *If I do X for the company, I will receive Y.* Associate all of your goals and achievements with a timeframe. If you have been promised that you will run the company *someday,* you may never live to see it.

SELF-PRESERVATION

Someone needs to know what you're doing

AS A GENERAL RULE your work won't speak for itself. *You* must speak for yourself.

Others will try to take credit for your work, even those who seem to have good intentions. You can really help yourself by making sure that managers and supervisors in your organization understand the effort you put into your job and the results you produce. A bit of modest bragging will not only help you come promotion time but it will also help discredit any attacks levied against you.

If management doesn't know you or your work ethic, they will naturally question any adverse information they hear about you. If they are familiar with you and your work, negative stories about you will be quickly dismissed as rumor.

Provide the right amount of information about yourself, but don't beat your accomplishments to death. Too many trips to the boss's office will annoy him or her, and may work against you.

THE BOMBER

"Have you heard?"

THERE IS ALWAYS SOMEONE who wants to deliver breaking news. I call this person the Bomber because they want to drop a bomb on everyone, hoping to generate some reaction.

The Bomber is looking for a sense of value and a bit of an ego boost. It makes them feel important if they know something you don't. The quickest way to identify one is to tell them a piece of news that should be kept confidential and see how long it takes for the story to get back to you. (Just make sure that the information you're leaking doesn't damn you or someone else.)

Once identified, Bombers can be useful. If you need to make an announcement, just tell the Bomber and ask him not to tell anybody. You probably won't have to issue a memo—the Bomber will take care of that for you.

DELIVERING NEWS

They might as well hear it from you

WHENEVER POSSIBLE, be your own messenger.

Anytime people transmit information, they have an opportunity to influence how data is interpreted, to manipulate or omit data, and to present themselves or their situation in the best light possible. The messenger has a lot of power. Don't give up this power.

Management is bombarded with information from many different sources and it falls on their shoulders to filter through the constant data flow. Whether bad news or good news, it's in your best interest to deliver the info yourself, so you are certain the message you want to send gets delivered as intended. You won't be able to control management's reaction, but at least you'll have some influence over what info they receive.

EDUCATION

Better yourself

EMBRACE SELF-IMPROVEMENT whenever you can. Furthering your education helps you not only in your current job, but it can help you in your future employment as well.

Over the years I have worked with a great many people who did not understand basics about the operation of their company. This is fairly common so if this describes you, you are not alone. Know the organizational chart and reporting structures. Study and understand your company's financials. Financial data is the basis for many decisions, decisions that may very well affect your wallet.

You never know where your life may lead. Learn as much as you can along the way, even though what you're learning may not seem relevant at the time.

SELLING YOURSELF

Guess what? You're in sales

JUST AS CORPORATIONS sometimes give us sales pitches on their behalf, we must also sell our abilities and our ideas on our behalf. Whether you view it this way or not, all of us have played the sales role at one time or another. Selling yourself and your talents doesn't end with the interview process.

You will encounter a lot of different viewpoints throughout your career and you should be prepared to do some convincing. If you have a new idea about a product or direction for the company, make sure it's something you are passionate about. When you go in to pitch your idea to management, be prepared to defend your views. Also be prepared to receive criticism. Other people have a right to their opinions, so don't get defensive if someone disagrees with you. Management will challenge you simply to test your level of enthusiasm for the idea, and its viability. New markets and new products come with a lot of risk to the organization. There are a lot of variables to consider, and management wants to know you've thought about them. If you support your ideas with solid research and show some passion, management will be more likely to embrace your concept.

AUTHORITY

"Because I said so" doesn't work

HOW MANY TIMES during your growing-up years did your parents say, "Just do it because I said so." This didn't work very well then and it doesn't work well in the corporate world either.

People won't do everything you tell them to do just because you are the boss. It is your job to convince them that your path is the one they should follow.

It is important to get good buy-in from your employees in order for them to put their full efforts toward a project or task. Leadership is about being a good evangelist for the company. If people believe, they will follow. If they don't believe, they will fight you every step of the way. In fact, they will go out of their way to make your life difficult and spread their misery around the organization, creating unrest in others as well.

Leading by authority works in the short-term but undermines your ability to lead in the long run.

THE TASKMASTER

"Do as I say, not as I do"

HAVE YOU EVER COME ACROSS someone at work who spends all of his time worrying about what everyone else is doing, while at the same time he complains that no one else in the company ever does anything and that he is saddled with all the work? This is the Taskmaster. Taskmasters are very quick to assign tasks to other people to avoid doing anything.

The Taskmaster constantly works to create the perception that he is so busy that he just couldn't possibly work one more thing into his day. In reality he has a lazy streak a mile wide and he works harder to get out of work than most of us do to get our work done.

As soon as a task is completed, somehow the Taskmaster is there to take the credit for getting it done. Beware of him. Keep him at a distance, or you will spend your days doing his job.

HANDLING CONFLICT

Make the tough choices

PEOPLE ARE MORE LIKELY to respect you as leader if you create a positive environment for them to work in. This is not an easy task. It is not only dependent on your attitude, but on others' around you as well.

People tend to emphasize negative things in the workplace over positive things. Whoever said "One bad apple can spoil the whole barrel" must have been a manager. One negative person or event can tear down months of motivation in minutes.

Evaluate the people working in your department or on your project. Do the personalities work well together? If a team member isn't on board with the task or project, make an effort to correct the problem right away. Don't give problems like these an opportunity to fester.

Some people cannot or will not get on board. Don't spend an inordinate amount of time trying to convince them to join in. Give them an opportunity to correct their negative attitude, but if they persist, remove them from the group or project. There are not enough hours in the day to convert someone who has convinced herself that she doesn't want to follow your plan.

EMPOWERMENT

Let them do their jobs

EMPOWERMENT—ENABLING PEOPLE to make decisions with minimal direction and trusting their judgment—is a good thing. It allows you to delegate tasks and helps your group run more efficiently. It makes your life easier, and improves your employees' levels of satisfaction.

Empowerment runs downstream. It is most effective when you've developed solid relationships above and below you.

Your superiors must understand the concept and be willing to pass authority on to you before you can pass it on to others. Make sure you have developed strong ties with management and that they trust you to make sound decisions. Will they respect the chain of command?

Employee inquiries and complaints should be directed back to you, not management. Otherwise, those you have empowered may think that you no longer have value and their egos will take over. They will try to take you out of the loop, and will go directly to management themselves.

If you've developed solid relationships with your subordinates and they trust you, you will have some protection against someone who becomes power hungry and tries to bypass you. Well-established leadership will help you manage any conflicts that arise.

Finally, empowerment is most powerful when it is shared among people with a common goal. Individual goals may not be identical, but if the whole group is moving in the same direction, stay out of each other's way and watch the magic happen.

THE COMPANY LINE

It doesn't exist for your benefit

ALL TOO OFTEN today's employees are concerned only about themselves and advancing their personal agendas. I have interviewed hundreds of potential employees and the same scenario rings true. It is all about what the company can do for them. Everything seems to be ME ME ME ME ME!

Even people fresh out of college are asking for huge salaries, long vacations, and exorbitant benefit packages. American corporations seem to have become the land of entitlement where people expect to be highly compensated before they have provided one penny of value to the company.

Throughout your career, evaluate what value you bring to a company. Management takes a risk by hiring you. Ask for fair compensation, but don't price yourself out of the market. There are limits on what a corporation can afford to pay you regardless of what you are asking for. Employment is a two-way street so make sure you are giving something for what you get.

DETAILS

Know what the contract says

ALL OF US HAVE SIGNED legal documents at some point in our lives. Did you ever stop to consider what they mean and whom they protect? When someone hands you a pen and says, "Here, sign this," read it before you sign it. Their legal document has been drafted to protect them, not you.

The most important thing to remember about contracts is that all parties are happy the day they are signed. If you want provisions added to a contract, do it before the deal is closed. Any changes after the closing can't be enforced, and if you challenge the agreement, you are likely to be at odds with the other party.

Protect yourself, even if it means walking away from the table until you get the agreement you want. This is a very difficult thing to do—especially if the contract in question is an employment agreement for a new job you really want—but walking away may be necessary.

Any details that are omitted from the contract can be costly. You may trust the other party when they say, "It didn't make the contract but we'll make good on your request anyway." Don't count on it. People forget these agreements quickly, especially if conflict arises. If they don't forget the agreement altogether, they will likely claim selective memory.

As they say, "The devil is in the details," so pay attention. Bottom line is don't sign any agreement unless you are satisfied with all provisions in the document. Whenever possible, have your own attorney draft a contract to protect you.

THE LAWYER

"That's against the law"

THE LAWYER THINKS they know it all, from contracts to divorce and everything in between. They have no formal legal training; everything they know about the law they learned from a Hollywood movie or afternoon TV talk show.

The Lawyer wants to give you legal advice. Don't take it. The law has nothing to do with right, wrong, or personal opinions, but the Lawyer doesn't recognize this distinction. If you have a legal problem, consult a qualified attorney and not the water cooler lawyer.

DOCUMENTATION

Cover your ass

NOT ONLY DO WE NEED to make sure we cover ourselves from a legal perspective, but we also need to cover our asses day-to-day. The best way to do this nowadays is to save all e-mail and electronic data that is available to you. If you have ever received an e-mail from someone asking you to confirm something, that person is likely covering her ass. This is not a bad thing and in many cases can clear up any confusion later.

Even the most obscure e-mail may be relevant at a later date. Disk space is cheap compared to the trouble it may save you.

IDEAS

Take risks with new ideas

NEW IDEAS DRIVE our economy, our workforce, and help us evolve. Without innovative thinking, we would still be back in the Stone Age. Don't be afraid to try new things even if some of your ideas fail.

When you come up with a new idea, try to poke holes in it yourself. See if you can figure out any reasons it won't work. If after doing so you still think it's feasible, let others critique it and see if the idea still holds water.

Keep in mind that the idea may be new to you, but others may have already tried it. Do some research to see if anyone has tested it or anything like it. If you find someone has tried it, look at their progress and try to understand why the idea may have succeeded or failed. Try to learn from others' mistakes. This can keep you from wasting valuable time and resources. Just because others have tried and failed does not mean that it is a bad idea. Most ideas fail due to the lack of a solid business plan or the inability to execute the plan.

If your new idea involves new products or markets, proceed with caution. You may be trying to penetrate a market that your competitors have seemingly ignored. There may be a very good reason why they decided not to play in that sandbox. Maybe there are some barriers to entry or legal issues that you are not aware of. Maybe they tried it and found that the idea wasn't profitable for them, so they got out.

So do some research to support your idea. Make sure it is financially viable. Some ideas may look good on a small scale but lose their viability when you roll them out to the masses. If your idea can pass these tests, it will be much easier to sell to management.

BALANCE

Get off the treadmill

WE ALL WANT TO do a good job and earn praise for our hard work. At the same time we need to set limits and make sure that our time and expertise are deployed effectively.

If you find that you spend an inordinate amount of time doing tasks for other people and that you get assigned to project after project with the same staff, you could be picking up someone else's slack. You may hear phrases like, "I always assign you the tough jobs because I know you deliver," or, "You're the one for the job." If so, it may be because you do a bang-up job, but it also may mean that the person assigning you these tasks may not want to do them personally. They would rather burn up your time than theirs.

Learn how to set limits and boundaries. Don't be afraid to say no. (If you're doing such a great job, they can't afford to get rid of you anyway.) If you don't set limits, you will find yourself working on a perpetual treadmill.

You should be properly compensated for your efforts. You're winning the race—claim the prize! If others make all the money but put in very little effort, go somewhere else and work for people who are willing to share the wealth.

WARFARE

Pick your battles

MOST OF US HAVE A TENDENCY to try to fix everything. Before you go out and do that, make sure it's a battle worth fighting.

Objectively assess the problem and determine if it is worth the effort to fix it. There are a few fundamental questions you must ask yourself: Is it worth my time and effort to fix the problem? Is fixing the problem really going to change things?

How many times have you heard, "It's just the principle of the thing," or, "This just isn't right!" Fighting for principle or to make things right in someone else's eyes often gets you nowhere. You must ask yourself if the opinions you are trying to change are really that important. If the answer is yes, then the battle is worth fighting and your time will be well spent.

When you try to tackle a large problem pick your battles. You may have to concede a few things along the way in order to reach your goal.

THE KNOW-IT-ALL

"Don't bother, I know this already"

SOME PEOPLE ACT like they know everything. To me this is a dangerous mindset. A statement such as, "Don't bother, I know this already," tells me that the person I'm talking to has stopped growing as an employee and probably as a person as well.

The Know-It-All will frustrate you to no end. The best way to deal with this type of person is to pass them by. Continue your own program of self-improvement and add value where you can within the company. Soon you will be out in front of the Know-It-All and you will leave them behind.

CHANGE

Don't fix what isn't broken

IN ALL MY YEARS in the corporate world there is one thing that I have never understood: Why do companies fix things that aren't broken? I am not saying that change is a bad thing, but lots of great initiatives get screwed up for the sake of change.

The only reason to change something is to make it better than it was previously. The goal is improvement.

What are your goals? Are they measurable? In other words, when your initiative is over, will you be able to tell a difference? If you can tell a difference, will it be because of the change you put in place or because of some other event? Put a time limit on your goals so you don't chase a bad idea longer than you should. If you haven't achieved your goal over a certain period of time, don't dismiss your efforts as futile immediately. Take an objective look at your findings and see if the trends are headed in the right direction. If they are, then you may want to test the change a little longer or maybe it needs a little tweaking.

The point here is, don't change things for the sake of change. Change them for the sake of improvement.

DIRECTION

You either ride the bus or drive it

IN THE GAME OF LIFE, there are those who ride on the bus and those who drive it. Either seat is okay; there are a lot of things to be said for both positions. However, you can't do both. How many people do you know who sit in the back of the bus and bitch about where it's going?

Don't complain about where the bus is going unless you are prepared to drive it. If you are the driver, you had better have a goal in mind and a map for getting there. A lot of people may be trying to get to the same place you are, so be prepared for some roadblocks along the way.

SELF-DECEPTION

Some people are busy doing nothing

SOME PEOPLE GET SO WRAPPED UP in the game that they forget why they are playing. I call it "busy doing nothing."

If you ask someone how their day went and they say, "I've been busy," ask them what they were doing. Chances are, their response is, "Nothing," or, "A lot of stuff." Really, how productive have they been? If they can't remember anything specific that they accomplished that day, then they probably can't get out of their own way. It's easy to get caught up doing nothing all day since there is always a lot of nothing to be done. The question is, are we getting any closer to our goals?

Stay focused on the big picture. Empower yourself and budget your time accordingly. Drive your job—don't let it drive you. Above all, keep things simple. Don't make your life any more complicated than it is already. Others will try and do that for you.

SELF-CONTROL

It's not personal

I AM SURE YOU HAVE HEARD this before but it's worth mentioning again. Try not to get your personal feelings and beliefs involved in business. Nothing good can come from this. You will wind up doing one of two things. Either you will make poor decisions based on your emotions or you will leave yourself open to adversaries who will play on your feelings.

Some of the most constructive meetings I have had over the years might have appeared very destructive to an outsider. My opponent and I fought, yelled, argued, and swore at each other. In the end, decisions were made and we went out for a beer together. It wasn't personal. If someone disagrees with your business plan, it is the plan they have a problem with. It is not a personal attack on you.

We all have emotions and we all get pissed off from time to time. If you are having a bad day, try not to make any decisions that are born of emotion. If someone sends you an e-mail that infuriates you, wait a day and sleep on it before you respond. You will be glad you did. Your carefully considered response will be more rational and productive than one driven by your initial reaction.

THE SOCIAL WORKER

"What's wrong?"

THE SOCIAL WORKER WANTS to get involved in everyone's personal lives and coach them through hard times or crises. The funny thing about the Social Worker is that their life is typically a dysfunctional disaster. It makes them feel good to hear about other peoples' problems because it makes them feel better about their own.

As a general rule, make every effort to keep your personal and professional lives separate. Try not to bring your problems to work or to get someone at work to help you solve them. If you need help, seek the advice of a professional and not the Social Worker unless you want your life to be as dysfunctional as theirs.

INTUITION

Gut instinct isn't always wrong

I BELIEVE ALL OF US HAVE a certain amount of intuition. At one time or another we have a "feeling" about some event in our lives. The feeling may be good or bad, but we know that our gut instinct is right.

Good intuition in the business world can be your guardian angel. If it feels like someone is up to no good, they probably are. In most cases you will find that your initial instinct about someone is usually correct. Keep that instinct in mind as you work with them and always remember how you felt that first day. Some people may turn out to be better than you thought, but this is rare. Stick to your convictions!

ASPIRATIONS

Be careful what you wish for

DREAMS AND ASPIRATIONS drive us all and contribute to our success. It is a good feeling to achieve great things but we need to be on the same page in regard to the things we think we are getting.

Make sure that your aspirations are in line with reality. You may think that the big promotion you want will come with a healthy pay raise and wonderful perks. In truth, the promotion may include very little increase in pay but many more hours. You don't need this kind of disappointment in your life. You will get enough of that from other people. Make sure what you are going after is really what you want.

TRAVEL

You'll earn every one of those million miles

SOME CORPORATE JOBS REQUIRE extensive travel. It is a common belief that company travel is all glitz, glamour, and vacations on somebody else's nickel. Nothing could be further from the truth.

Corporate travel means you'll be in a multitude of airports, hotels, restaurants, and conference rooms. After awhile, they all look the same. And the food sucks.

If you are considering a career that involves corporate travel, keep in mind that travel time is not included in your work week. Expect to spend forty to sixty hours a week working plus travel time. Travel makes for a lot of late nights, early mornings, and catch-up time on the weekends.

Another popular myth is that all of the frequent flyer miles you accumulate will enable you to travel on your own time for free. I can tell you from years of experience that none of the frequent travel programs live up to their advertising. They hold no real value to the serious traveler, so don't waste your time routing through ten different cities just to log miles. At the end of the day you will likely lose interest in traveling altogether. A great vacation for you will be spending some time at home.

THE JOB

Love the job

WE'VE TALKED ABOUT A LOT of things that can help you in your career but one thing we haven't talked about is the job itself. At some point in your career you have to ask yourself, "Do I love this job?" You may love the money you generate or the lifestyle your job allows, but do you love the job itself?

I've heard a lot of people say that they love their job but in the next sentence say, "Thanks, God. It's Friday!" If you can't wait to get out of work and go home each day you probably don't love your job. Really loving your job usually means that you would do it for no money and do it as often as possible.

Why is this so important? Well, consider this fact the next time you are frustrated with work. You spend approximately 30 percent of your life working. Therefore, if you are unhappy with your job, you will spend 30 percent of your life unhappy. Life is too short for that.

Now I am not saying that we can all grab a set of golf clubs and go make millions on the pro golf tour but we can find something we love to do. Some of the wealthiest people I know don't think of their jobs as work. They can't wait for Monday to roll around so they can get back to it. How many of us can really say that?

THE TEACHER

"Let me show you what to do"

THE TEACHER IS A VERY IMPORTANT person in your organization. Adequate training is in short supply, and consequently a lot of workers aren't confident about what they are doing. Teachers go out of their way to make sure that employees are comfortable with their roles and have opportunities to move up.

Unfortunately the Teacher is becoming a rare breed. Nowadays, people are content to let their fellow employees struggle. They figure that a floundering coworker is no threat to their job, which gives them a feeling of security.

If you have Teachers in your midst, do whatever you can to keep them around. They are invaluable to you and the company.

LIFE

The game will soon be over

I AM SURE YOU HAVE HEARD this somewhere along the way: Don't forget to have a life. It's good to be committed to the company and corporate accomplishments are rewarding, but when all is said and done, a lifetime goes by too fast.

I'm the first to admit that I neglected this maxim. It seems like yesterday I was fresh out of college and looking forward to a long career ahead of me. I would look at those folks who were twenty years in and think they were ancient. Now I'm the old man after twenty years.

Not only should we evaluate where we are in life, but we should also evaluate where we are in our career. You will find that your wants and needs change over time and things that may have been important to you in years past don't have much meaning now. Do a gut check on your career every year and see if it still satisfies you. Switching careers is a challenge, but it's not impossible.

Try not to take your job home with you. This not only makes things more stressful for you but it also puts undue pressure on those around you. I am a firm believer that you get what you give. If you are happy, those around you will be happy as well.

Both your home and your career life will be helped out if you live within your means. You know all that stuff you buy? It's just stuff. Having no debt and reasonable material goals not only reduces stress, but it also makes it possible for you to take advantage of career opportunities that may be less lucrative but much more fulfilling. As a rule I always have enough resources set aside that I can survive at my current lifestyle for one year without any income. You may not need to set aside this much, but having substantial cash reserves gives you freedom and flexibility.

AMBITION

Responsibility has a price

DO YOU WANT TO BE RESPONSIBLE for the success or failure of your company? If so, move up the ladder. Do you want to go home at five every day and forget about work until the next morning? Then moving up the ladder is not for you.

Most people want to move up the ladder because that's what they've been told they should do. In reality, some people want to move up and others don't. The really important thing is that you do your job to the best of your ability and you are happy doing it.

If you are planning to move up the ladder, remember that staying on the top rungs can be harder than getting there. Someone is always trying to come up behind you. It may even be a friend who helped you achieve your status, only because getting you one rung closer to the top got them one rung closer also. So be prepared for a few battles when you get there.

TIME MANAGEMENT

Half-ass doesn't count

TIME IS THE MOST PRECIOUS commodity we have. We need to learn how to get the most out of every day and be as efficient as possible. The best advice I can offer is to prioritize and concentrate on what matters.

Ask yourself if the task you are currently working on is relevant to the big picture of what you are trying to accomplish. Don't get tied up in things that are of little or no importance just because they need to be done. Your time may be better spent somewhere else.

Most people fail at time management because they want to do everything. If you try to do everything you may very well get it all done, but it will be done half-ass. Give the important tasks the time they require. Push the low priorities aside if you must.

Another time waster I have seen people struggle with over the years is performing a task several times. Complete the task once if possible. If you start working on something and set it aside you will spend even more time catching up on that task when you come back to it. Get it done the first time. You will be surprised how much time you really have.

PERSONAL DIRECTION

Have an exit strategy

YOUR GOALS SHOULD BE IN line with the company's goals in order to create synergy with your employer. How do you determine if there is alignment and when do you part ways if there isn't?

If you have been promised certain things or are expecting a specific direction from the company and they seem to be going a different way, ask for some changes to be made in order to correct the course. Attach realistic timelines to the changes. Try not to set your expectations too high; companies don't change overnight. Don't work with just one deadline but recommend a schedule of improvements over time. Think about your own timeline and determine what your strategy will be if the changes don't happen. Looking at these in parallel will allow you to determine if the organization has made progress and at the same time force you to develop an exit strategy if things don't work out. As the deadlines come and go, monitor them for indications of improvement.

Like a bad marriage, some people keep expecting things to change and they never do. Frustration builds, and eventually someone says, "I quit." Make sure you have an exit strategy in place and know when to get out.

FATHER TIME

"This was all farmland when I was growing up"

IF YOU HAVE EVER SAT on the corporate porch and talked about the good 'ol days then you've met Father Time. He is the one who remembers how everything used to be. You will hear about his years of service at the company or in the industry on a regular basis. This may be a good thing if he has been there for thirty years and is now running the company. But if he has stayed in the same position for that length of time, try to steer clear of his advice.

Father Time's best asset is experience. He is adept at solving problems and there isn't much he hasn't seen. However, his experience must intersect with new technology and methods in order to maintain its value and relative viability.

Father Time has a tendency to hoard information. When he leaves the company, he will likely take all of his experience and knowledge with him. Don't let him get too comfortable in his job. Try to change things up in everyone's work environment, including Father Time's and your own. This will help break up mundane jobs for some people, and will also encourage information sharing. The last thing you want is to have Father Time—or anyone else, for that matter—walk off with all their knowledge in tow.

PICKING AN INDUSTRY

Know how far you can go

SO HOW DO YOU PICK your career path? You must first evaluate your personal goals. Look at your short-term and long-term goals to determine if they are in alignment with the career path you are interested in. For example, if your goal is to become very wealthy, look at the highest-paid individual in the profession that interests you. If that person isn't making the kind of money you hope for, then don't invest twenty years trying to get to the top of that industry. I have talked to hundreds of people who said they would like to be rich, yet they are usually working in a career or industry where it is never going to happen. It's not all about money; just make sure that the career path you have chosen supports whatever it is you want to get out of life.

KNOWING THE INDUSTRY

Find the best in the business

ONCE YOU HAVE CHOSEN a career path, find out what organization is the leader in that industry. If possible, work for them, especially if it is early in your career. This will allow you access to a lot of experience in the industry and you can learn from others' mistakes and successes.

Other companies in the industry will always be playing catch up instead of living on the cutting edge and developing new and exciting products or services. The industry leader is typically well-known and doesn't have to prove itself every time like the underdogs of the industry do. It is much better to work for the company that makes the leading mouse trap than the one that claims they have made a better one.

HUMILITY

Shut up and listen

WE ALL EXPECT PEOPLE to listen to our ideas and learn from our experience. We should also listen to others and learn from them. Having an opportunity to speak with someone who has already been down the road you are traveling is priceless. This interaction can save you exponential amounts of time and money.

Experienced people don't claim to be any smarter than you are. Rather, they can tell you what might succeed or fail because they have seen it before. If you don't know what you don't know, then seek out some experienced advice. A mentor can warn you about things you may never have considered and keep you from being blindsided by unforeseen events or costs. As hard as it may be, the first step is to admit to yourself that you don't know everything.

INTERNAL CUSTOMERS

Everyone is a customer

MOST OF US THINK of customers as the people or companies who buy our product. In reality we have internal customers as well. Anyone who depends on you or your department to provide information or to complete a certain task is your customer. They are the consumers of your product and should be treated as such. Take care of them—exceed their expectations—as if they were paying directly for your product or service and you will have a much better working relationship with them.

JACK-OF-ALL-TRADES

"I can help you with that"

JACK-OF-ALL-TRADES IS A GENUINELY good person, one who is very helpful to his fellow employees. Jack gets his nickname because he's willing to help with anything, even if he knows very little about the subject at hand.

He may get involved in different tasks because he is looking for a distraction from his current job or project. He may have a short attention span, which makes it a struggle for him to focus on a single task for a long period of time. Sometimes this is a good thing, but it can also create an inefficient environment.

For example, perhaps the company just bought a new software platform. As people learn how to use the software, they will undoubtedly have questions and get stuck from time to time. This is where Jack comes in. Jack spends a lot of time running around the office trying to fix software problems that he doesn't really know much about instead of calling experts who could solve the problem more quickly. Before long, Jack has burned up his entire day solving problems for other people and he's lost focus on his own role.

Don't become a Jack. It may feel good to be the go-to person and head problem solver and you will help a lot of people, but you will do so at the expense of your own responsibilities. Leave the answers to the experts.

AUTOMATION

Adapt quickly to new systems

UNLESS YOU HAVE BEEN LIVING on the moon for the past several years, you have been involved in a system change or two or twelve. People tend to shy away from change. It's human nature to do so.

Automation exists to make our work easier, so embrace the changes and use them to your advantage. Focus on what will make you more productive. How many times have you spent an entire day working on a report that you had to present to the company? Wouldn't you rather have a system that can provide you with the report in five minutes and spend the entire day working on the overall presentation? So be flexible and stay ahead of the curve when it comes to new technology. Doing so will make your job easier and most importantly increase your value to the organization.

POSITIVE INFLUENCE

Create a great place to work

WHEN IT COMES to the work environment, negative influences seem to win out over positive ones. There are enough negative influences on employees today without us creating more.

Maintain a positive attitude and it will rub off on others. Listen to suggestions from others and don't just dismiss them. Smile. Embrace changes and new ideas. Compliment others on their work. Help others without them having to ask. Keep gossip to a minimum—in fact, don't pass it on at all.

If you encounter someone who spreads negativity, try to turn it around and don't add any fuel to the fire. Your superiors will appreciate any help you can provide in the effort to create a better work environment.

PRIORITIZING

Choose wisely

THERE ARE MORE THINGS to do in life than we will ever have time for. It is very important that we prioritize well in order to be more effective in our professional and personal lives.

Prioritizing is simple if you take an objective look at your daily tasks. Try to look at things as a whole. Then evaluate the individual tasks as they relate to the entire project or task. Rate the items that need to be completed. Focus on the most important ones first and so on. This will make your day much more productive and will get you closer to the completion of your project.

RETURN ON INVESTMENT

What's the ROI?

RETURN ON INVESTMENT (ROI) drives almost everything in the business world. It is not only a measure of money or capital invested, but of time and resources as well. The company measures its ROI on you. You should measure the ROI on yourself as well.

None of us have the time to do everything, so we are faced with trade-offs every day. Do I do this or that? Focus on the items that use your time and resources most effectively. Ask yourself, "What is the ROI?" before you dive in.

THE CLEANER

"I'll clean up the mess"

THE CLEANER IS A CLOSE COUSIN to the Repairman. They clean up mess after mess just so they can tell everyone that they did it. Their favorite phrase is, "That's another mess I'll have to clean up."

Their compulsion allows Cleaners to create the perception that they are saviors and the company can't live without them. They are like a painter who works without a drop cloth. Sooner or later, paint is going to get on the carpet and it will have to be cleaned up.

Once Cleaners "do their thing," rest assured that everyone in the company will know that they did it, and how long it took them. They will also make sure everyone knows who made the mess.

FOLLOW-UP

Be true to your word

HOW MANY TIMES have you had someone tell you they were going to do something and they didn't do it? There is nothing more frustrating than people who don't follow up on their word.

Lack of follow-up can create a lot of negative press for you in a hurry. The first thing that will happen is you will lose all credibility. Any further promises you make will be ignored or dismissed. Your value as an employee will quickly erode and others will have the perception that you are not doing your job. It will also make it easy for them to take shots at you and blame you for their failures.

Don't fall into this trap. Make sure you close all loops and follow up on everything. *Sending a text message is not a follow-up!* Even with the latest and greatest digital communications gadgets, things still get lost in the mail. Take the time to make a call.

COMMUNICATION

Build personal relationships

COMMUNICATING WITH PEOPLE is an opportunity not only to transfer information, but also to build relationships with them at the same time. With all the forms of electronic communication available today our conversations are becoming more and more impersonal. Not only are texts and e-mails inefficient and sometimes carried to ridiculous extremes, they are also costing us our personal relationships.

Text and e-mail exchanges can take days to get problems resolved; a live conversation can get things resolved in minutes. So if you intend to text your way through work all day, don't plan to work for me. I need someone who will interact with people and resolve problems. If you can't interact with people directly, you have no value.

PLANNING

Have a plan

A LOT OF PEOPLE HAVE NO IDEA what they intend to accomplish on any given workday. If this describes you, maybe it means that your job is driving you when instead you should be driving your job.

How many times have you gone to work and been swamped with tasks that others have asked you to do? Being busy isn't necessarily being productive. In reality you may be improving others' productivity but not your own.

Good planning can help. Create a plan, work to it, and set timelines for tasks. Make sure the timelines are realistic and communicated to the group. We all have other things "come up," so fit them in when you can but try not to deviate from your plan. Remember that someone else's emergency is not necessarily yours. Try to set expectations for when you will respond to others' requests. Replying instantly to every e-mail message is not necessarily a wise thing to do. Your work may become backlogged and you will gain a reputation as someone who can put out other people's fires.

Be proactive, create a plan, and leave the fires to someone else.

DEADLINES

Deadlines aren't evil

"I'M SORRY, BUT I NEED THIS tomorrow." How many times have you heard that one? Deadlines are a necessary evil. They are designed to motivate behavior, but don't you wish you would be rewarded for meeting them instead of facing certain doom if you don't? Try to think about this next time you set a deadline.

Don't just consider your own schedule when you assign them. Make sure they are reasonable. Most projects fall behind schedule because someone was too optimistic about the completion date. Always try to incorporate extra time into the schedule to compensate for emergencies.

Deadlines are useful not only at work, but in our personal lives as well. Most of us do not set deadlines for ourselves and we should. How many times have you said, "I've been meaning to do that," or, "One of these days, when I have time." If you don't set your own deadlines and plan your own projects they likely will never happen. Make time for yourself and try to be as efficient at home as you are at work. You will meet more of your personal goals and have time for those things you've been "meaning" to do.

THE WAKEBOARDER

"Watch out—coming through!"

CHANCES ARE YOU HAVE WORKED with the Wakeboarder. This person usually has an outgoing personality and is a bit of a networker. However, he doesn't network to socialize or name-drop. Instead, he's on the lookout for ways to distribute his workload throughout the organization.

You know the Wakeboarder has an impending deadline because you see him consume a lot of resources. Take a walk around the office and you will likely see staff rallying to help this person complete his task or project. Although Wakeboarders are typically good employees and produce high-quality finished products, they leave a wake a mile wide as coworkers bust their asses to help them complete their projects.

JOB SATISFACTION

Know when it's time to move on

I CAN'T TELL YOU the number of times I have heard someone say, "If I owned this place, things would be different." Let's assume for a minute that you have all of the resources required to buy the company that you work for. Would you? How many members of management would you remove from the company if you owned it?

If the answer to the first question is no and the answer to the second question is some or all of them, then you should really evaluate whether or not you should continue to work there. Unless you have the resources to buy the company, ownership and management problems will never change. So get the hell out of there!

MOTIVATION

Know what's important to people

THE KEY TO KEEPING A STAFF motivated is simple: Find out what motivates them. This is a relatively easy task and can be done within the context of a simple conversation. Ask people what is important to them and what they like to do in their off time. They will typically reveal what motivates them early in the conversation.

Once you understand the motivational forces in a person's life, you can set up a reward system for a job well done. Just remember that you are dealing with individuals who are driven by different things. Don't make the mistake of rewarding all employees the same way. If you do so, your motivational plan will probably fail.

SELF-IMPROVEMENT

Evaluate the system

IT'S IMPORTANT TO IMPROVE yourself from an educational standpoint, but you can also improve the processes you and your coworkers employ. As you work through your daily tasks, be aware of how much time you spend doing them, especially those that are repetitive. Can you perform these duties less often and still get a quality job done? How many people are needed to accomplish the task? What are their time requirements? These are some of the questions you should ask yourself daily.

Companies are always looking for ways to make day-to-day operations more efficient, ways that may translate into cost savings for the organization. If you can help improve efficiency, the company will value you more, and you may find a path for advancement. When you do discover something that will help the company, don't forget to "blow your own horn" a little so management is aware of your efforts.

THE SUPERHERO

"I can do it all"

THE SUPERHERO IS THE OPPOSITE of the Wakeboarder. They try to do everything themselves with very little delegation. They live by the motto "Sometimes it's just easier to do it yourself." You often find this personality in a sales or service role, someone who does a lot of work in the field.

This personality is very efficient but still winds up working long hours because they tend to take on too much. Often, the Superhero doesn't trust others to deliver the same result that they would. They have a bit of a control problem.

Encourage them to let people help them. This will be hard at first, especially if there is a kink in your company's support process. But once the Superhero has learned to let go, he will be much happier in his role and will produce higher quality work in the long run.

SELF-EMPLOYMENT

You don't have to be an employee forever

IF YOU HAVE EVER CONSIDERED starting your own business, you may be closer than you think. Thousands of businesses have been spawned through employer–employee relationships.

There are any number of tasks that are not cost-effective for one company to support with direct staff. That's one reason companies outsource certain functions. You may be able to create a profitable business by offering a desired service to several companies—including the one you work for right now.

Take a look at what you do for the company every day. Look for things the company must do to survive but are not part of their product or service. If you think there are several companies that might require the services you've identified, you may have the makings for a business.

This could be a win–win scenario for you and the company. The company will save money by outsourcing to you, and you may build a profitable business connecting with others as well.

I hope you have enjoyed reading this book as much as I enjoyed writing it. I wish you the best of luck in your career and hope you achieve the success you always dreamed of. If you would like to share your comments or you have a "Corporate Bullshit" story of your own to tell please go to www.corporatebullshitguide.com and pass them along. I am always interested in the challenges that people are facing out there in the world and how we can help make your job more enjoyable and fulfilling.